Soaring With Burnt Wings

Lessons in love, life, laughter and surviving unimaginable loss

By Elizabeth Leanne

Author's Disclaimer

However, it is still very likely that others who were involved in Cam's and my life during this time will have different memories of the exact same experiences. Our individual perspectives have altered and interpreted the events both as they occurred, but especially as time has gone on. In no way do I claim that my recollection is more valid or accurate than another's. But everything written is my truth, my reality, my memory of these beautiful and devastating experiences. That is all I can offer you. My side of the story; as I remember and lived it.

Dedication

To my best friend, love, and late husband, Cameron. Thank you for teaching me what it means to live and live well. You opened my heart and eyes. You taught me to love myself and how to accept love from others. You opened my wings and set me free. Thank you for the thousands of seconds I had with you; I'll treasure them all forever. Thank you for always believing in me. I finally believe in myself, darling; and will now soar higher than the mountains we loved to climb. I've transformed into the beautiful butterfly you always knew me to be. You unleashed my confidence. Thank you. I would have followed you anywhere; done anything for you, but you went the one place you made me promise I would not follow on my own accord. I hated that promise and yet, now am forever grateful for it, as it has given me a second chance. I dedicate this book to you with complete adoration and love, as it is our story and would not exist without you.

Table of Contents

Prequel:
Waking In A Nightmare

I awake with a start. My body knows what my mind cannot yet accept; what it cannot comprehend. Slowly I open my eyes. It's as if somehow I know that once I open my eyes there will be no more denying the reality in which I now live. I look at my hand as if it belongs to someone else; wishing it belonged to someone else. My hand lying on the empty cold sheets. My hand reaching out as it has done thousands of times after a bad dream, yet this time it lays empty, untouched. Confusion begins to fill my sleepy mind, and then the memories begin to slam into me with such force my entire body revolts against me.

My mind screams *"no, no, no, please no!"*, pushes against the memories, against the truth. Absolute devastation consumes me, as I am reminded that the nightmare I awoke to escape has indeed become my reality. The day I dreaded has come. He is gone. I am alone. There is no turning back the clock. My love, my husband, my Cam has died.

I want to scream. I want to run, to escape this place, and all its memories. I want to die. But I do not move. I lie frozen, while silent tears leak from my eyes until finally sobs consume my body. Eventually, I learn to trick my mind by placing pillows around my sleeping form, so when I unconsciously reach for him, in my sleep, my hand touches the pillow and I, for some reason, do not wake. But I'm getting ahead of myself. There is always more to a story than solely devastation, and at times, in order to move forward, it is necessary to go backward. So, let us begin at the beginning; or at least Cameron's beginning.

Chapter One:
The Younger Years

On May 11, 1985, a squiggly little boy was born into the world. As with every being that is born, his future was unknown. Anything and everything was possible. His parents, like most, held him and felt his tiny heart beating, heard his endless wails, and prayed life would be easy on him; that they could protect him from all the pain and harm that they knew life could hand out. But even a parent's ability to love and protect their child has limits. Love, as I would later often say to Cam, is simply not enough.

Cam was the youngest of three children, and the only boy. He loved having two older sisters, not so much when he was living at home with them and growing up, but later as a teenager and young adult. Cam was very much in touch with his feminine side, and was almost more comfortable sitting around with a group of girls than he was with guys, particularly if it was a group of strangers. He attributed this to hanging out with his sisters and their friends so much.

Another gift he developed, from having two older sisters, was learning the importance of telling someone he cared about that he loved them. I marveled at how easily and frequently he told his family, me, my family, and even his friends that he loved them. When I questioned him about this, Cam laughed and said that his sisters would force him to tell them he loved them. Now it was just habit to tell those he loved how he felt. I'm so grateful for all the times I got to hear those three amazing words. Every boy needs a big sister to train them!

Cam was a sleep talker as am I. This often resulted in us talking to each other in our sleep. A few times, that we luckily laughed about later, we actually got into arguments while still sleeping and then would wake up confused by the other's yelling. We used to laugh that not only could we not stop talking while awake, but we were so connected that even unconsciously we had to stay in communication. There literally were not enough hours in a day to say all the things we wanted to say to each other.

In 1998, Cam started school at Foothills Academy where I had already been attending for four years. We became instant friends. He made me laugh like no one I had ever met before could. This was Cam's trademark. His incredible sense of humor and ability to say things at the perfect time to make a whole room break into laughter. Many times it was borderline to fully inappropriate, and I'm sure the teachers had a hell of a time trying not to laugh while reprimanding him at the same time. He dated a few of my friends in junior high, and I dated a couple of guys in the school, but Cam was my best guy friend. We talked every night on the phone, and once he started dating one of my best friends, he was adopted into our group as the token boy. Once again his comfort at being the only guy with a bunch of girls shone through. One day in my basement, we were all hanging out when we were about 15 and 16 years old. We decided that we would do Cam's makeup. Being the awesome sport he always was and, truth be told had to be in order to hang out with a girls' only group, he let us put mascara, eyeshadow, blush, and lipstick on him. To top it off, I got him to put on one of my mom's long red velvet dresses and a dark, long haired wig. He even let us take pictures, which I still have to this very day, and will forever treasure.

I have hundreds of memories of Cam and I, and the girls from our junior high days; yet I know that his time with us was only a fraction of his life during that time. He had friends from outside of school that I had heard the names of but never met, and obviously he had his family life. The stories that make up a life, make up a single year, are endless. One of my favorite memories of Cam, though at the time it was one of the more embarrassing moments we had together, was at his then-girlfriend's 16th birthday party. Once again, he was the only boy with all us girls. Her parents had rented a limo to take us to dinner and home again; which was a huge deal as many of us had never been in a limo before.

After dinner, the limo driver was driving us around town and I was standing out the window, being my crazy self, screaming and laughing. Cam reached over and lifted up my skirt so all the girls in the limo as well as himself could see my butt, in my lovely thong. Immediately, I clenched my bum cheeks and tried to get back in the limo or get my arms in to pull my skirt back down. But I was too late as I had been fully exposed.

Cam very matter-a-fact stated, "Wow, you have a really wrinkly ass!"

Yup, that one resulted in my checking my bum out in the mirror later on and wishing my instinct wasn't to clench!

In 2000, Cam decided to leave our school and go back in to the public system to be with his guy friends. He broke up with my friend at the urging of his friends because 'there would be so many options in high school'. At first we tried to stay in touch and hung out a few times together. I specifically remember the last time we hung out, and that I decided that I had to end our friendship.

Both of us were single, which was a first, since we had become friends years before. Cam was always very flirtatious and sexual. However, he had added a bit of extra kick to some of the things he was insinuating or saying. By this point I had had a crush on him for over a year, but he had never been available. Even if he had been, it would have been social suicide to date one of the girl's ex-boyfriends. As a hormone driven teenager, I did not trust myself to be able to keep our strict friendship boundaries if we kept hanging out, so I decided to walk away from our friendship. Once fate brought us back together again, I found out that Cam had liked me too, which was why he had been hitting on me so strongly the last time we hung out. He had been hurt and confused when I stopped calling or answering his calls.

4

I cried many tears over the loss of that friendship. However, I knew that with three years left with the same group of girls the rest of my school days would be a living hell if anything happened between Cam and me. I never replaced that friendship, and I thought of him every couple of months for years.

Later when we reconnected, Cam talked about his high school years, as well as the years afterwards. While there were amazing memories and things he laughed about, he often discussed how he went down the road of using drugs and drinking. After graduating from high school, he moved to New Brunswick to go to recording arts school. It was here that his anxiety reached its peak. Over the last couple of years of his life Cam did learn how to cope and manage anxiety for the most part. Although I wasn't around during his time in New Brunswick, Cam reported to me that he didn't want to leave his home. He would spend days on end in his room ordering pizza and beer to be delivered and playing World of War Craft to escape reality.

In hopes of breaking this cycle and starting fresh, he moved to Kelowna, British Columbia the following year and continued recording arts school there. At first this appeared to be a very good move for Cam. He made friends easily, started going to the gym, and really enjoyed school. Unfortunately, drugs and alcohol began to take precedence once more. We later spent hours where he would sit and tell me stories of different nights, parties, and various things he did, all while marveling that he somehow lived through it all.

After living in Kelowna for three years, he realized that if he didn't leave this was simply going to be his life. He called home and told his parents he was coming back to Calgary, packed up what he could fit in his truck and left the next day. That was September 2008. Relocating does not simply solve your problems; however, in his case, it was a step in the right direction. And little did he know at the time it was a step back to me.

Chapter Two:
All Fairy Tales Have Struggle

I still remember when I got the invite to join Facebook. It was February 2007. I was living in the Yukon again and relied on email to keep in touch with all my friends in Calgary. It seemed weird, but a few people I knew were joining so I thought I'd give it a try. I'm sure my Facebook story sounds very similar to others. The number of friends I had grew at a rapid rate those first two or three months and among them was Cam.

I remember the excitement of that friend request. I remember his profile picture perfectly; remember thinking how hot he had ended up being in the pool, shirtless and muscular. At that time he was living in Kelowna. We chatted on and off for a year and a half. Catching up on what the last 8 years had held for us, discussing what we were up to this weekend or that, mostly mindless banter. But, as we joked about it later, there was also a very flirtatious note to our messages.

Cam invited me to come visit him in Kelowna a few times, but I was always wary. Having had bad experiences with male friends not respecting my boundaries left me fearful of being alone with any man. Sadly Cam fell in this category. In the fall of 2007 I moved to Victoria and started seeing a counselor to work on these issues, as it was affecting my ability to enjoy and embrace life. So on December 11, 2008, when a number I did not recognize flashed on my cell phone 6 hours after my plane had landed in Calgary for a visit, I answered. I still remember the shock and excitement when the unknown caller said, "Hi this is Cam. Do you remember me from Foothills?"

I laughed because, of course, I remembered him. He had been my best friend and we had talked enough on Facebook that I didn't need reminding who he was. He admitted he had seen that I was going to be in Calgary and my cell number on a mutual friend's Facebook wall. He decided to call so we could get together, as he had moved back that fall. I can't tell it nearly as potently as he used to, but essentially over the next 20 minutes Cam managed to get me to go from agreeing to see him for a coffee the day before I flew out, to Saturday night (4 days away), and finally his coming to see me right then.

I still marvel at his ability to get this girl, who hadn't let herself be alone with a guy in over 3 years, and convince her to get together on the spot. It went against my very nature, my very planned and thought-out schedule. But as he rationalized, I was simply waiting for my mom to get off work and pick me up from my friend's condo. He only lived 10 minutes from where I was. Cam was many, many things and yes, one of them was a wonderful manipulator. I mean that in the most loving way possible, but he knew how to get what he wanted. And he wanted to hang out. As he later explained, he had 'creeped' my pictures, decided I had turned out better looking than in junior high, and that he wanted to see where it would go.

Neither of us expected it to go where it did. Right from the moment I opened the door and gave him a big hug, I knew something was different. I felt safe! I was alone with a guy and I felt safe. I also felt like no time had passed, as we immediately started teasing each other and joking just as we had 8 years prior. I went back to his mom's house where he was staying and we ate pizza, chatted and just laughed. It had been 3 and a half years since I had slept with a man, but that night I decided that if there was ever a time to break my celibacy, tonight with Cam might be it.

Now, I was rusty on flirting and giving the go ahead signals, but I'm pretty sure I was making it evident by leaning against him more and more on the couch, turning my head toward him and staying there longer, waiting for him to kiss me. Then it was after midnight and he hadn't made a move yet, though it was seemingly going in that direction. So I just bluntly stated, "I have a question. If we hook up tonight, is it going to ruin our friendship? Because I really like having you back in my life and it's not worth it to me to mess that up just for one night of fun."

Cam teased me about this for the rest of our days together. After that it took him over two hours to get the nerve up to kiss me. I'm sure that my asking a couple of times what was taking him so long didn't help at all, as he was nervous. Cam told me that he felt like he was 13 again and this was the first time he was going to kiss a girl but didn't know how to do it properly.

I won't go into details but he did kiss me and we did end my celibacy. Well, the next day he explained that the nervousness came from never having been with someone as straight forward as me, and that it had been over 5 years since he had had sex sober. It was a night of relived firsts, and as sappy as this sounds, we both agreed that we fell head over heels in love on that very first night. That love only grew as we learned more about each other, but it was not an easy fairy tale. No, I always said love was the easy part for us; it was everything else that was difficult.

I lived in Victoria and Cam lived in Calgary. I had no desire to ever move back to Calgary. I had promised myself when I left in 2006 that I would never return there; that the fast pace and money-hungry place was not for me. On day three of sleeping together; on day three of feeling my heart speeding down a one way track, I looked at him while we lay in bed and stated in my blunt manner that this was simply a fun hook up and wouldn't go any further. He agreed that the last thing he wanted was a long distance relationship, and we would have tons of fun over the next few days and then just remain friends. And then Cam threw in that if we still happened to be single when I next visited, we could meet up and have fun again. To which, of course, I readily agreed.

Already the intense attraction between us, which I can only describe to be like magnets, was setting in; we were already feeling the draw of the other, yet did not realize how intense this would become. All good intentions to simply have a fun Christmas fling began to get blurred as I went to his family pre-Christmas dinner, and he came to mine as some of his family would be gone on Christmas Day, so they were celebrating early as was my family. On day 7 he sent me a text while I was visiting a friend and hadn't seen him in almost 24 hours saying "I miss you. Is that weird?" I felt my heart swell and instantly knew I was in trouble; knew that I liked this boy more than a little fling; knew I didn't want it to end in two days. But I also knew I would never be the one to ask him to give distance a chance.

Saying goodbye to him on December 19th, the first of oh-so-many heart-wrenching goodbyes, was a strange mixture of "thank you for such a wonderful few days"; trying to be strong and acknowledge that this was now the end, and yet voicing that we both wanted to stay in contact. Asking if it was okay to stay in contact. We had no idea how to say goodbye after the nine days we had just had together. Nine days where everything else stopped, time stood still, and no one else mattered. Nine days where it was just Cam and me, craving each other's bodies, laughing uncontrollably, dancing around the living room together as if we were at the best party ever, was all that mattered. Nine days of complete and utter happiness.

Within 5 minutes of walking through the security gate at the airport, I heard my phone go off and a text came through from Cam reiterating how grateful he was we had reconnected and how much fun he had had, how much he already missed *his* goofball. Needless to say, we spent hours on the phone everyday while I visited my family in the Yukon, and on December 24th Cam told me that he knew we had agreed to not date, but he didn't care about the distance; he would rather have me as his girlfriend and only see me every few months than chance someone else getting me.

I agreed, much like everything with Cam where I was powerless to say no to him. I was completely infatuated with him and the fact that he wanted me left me feeling completely amazed.

On New Year's Eve a very drunk Cam called too late for my family to be happy about and I quickly threw myself out of bed to answer the phone, as I knew who it would be calling at such an hour. Sure enough it was Cam, and we talked in hushed voices. He went on about how his life had changed since I came into it only a few weeks earlier. And then he said those words from which there was never to be any going back: "I love you, I'm completely in love with you." I, of course, repeated them. And you know what? I meant them with every ounce of my body, more than I may have ever meant anything before. When you say those words and really mean them, there is a kind of reaction in your body, a pulsing, a warmth, a truth that is undeniable. I have never felt that with another person the way I did with Cam. I have come to accept that while I will likely love again, it will be a different love and this deep complete infatuation and unconditional love will likely never be mine again.

Years later, Cam marveled at how he had always had a feeling that he would end up marrying someone from Junior or High School and how very happy he was that it was me. We often laughed about how we both had crushes on each other through grade 7, 8 and 9 while we were best friends and dating other people. We marveled at how things happen for a reason and how glad we were that we never acted on our crushes because had we dated and broken up previously, we might not have been as inclined to try dating later on.

I remember the intense attraction I felt towards him even as a young teenager, yet he was always dating one of my best girlfriends and so there was no option but to stuff those feelings. And when he became available, I ended our friendship promptly for I knew I would be powerless to not succumb to my longing, and that it would have been social suicide to date another girl's ex-boyfriend in my small high school. But now there was no one and nothing standing between us, and so we were drawn together like a moth to the light. However, sometimes that blind attraction results in one getting a bit burnt.

Denial is a powerful thing, especially if you have a vested interest. So when my social work brain, which just happened to be doing a practicum at an addictions treatment center, started to send warnings to my head over heels heart, there was a lot of inner conflict. My first indication could or should have been when Cam told me I was the first person in 5 years he slept with sober. He was only 23, so I made excuses. And then there was the fact that he was drunk more often than sober throughout Christmas and New Year's, but so were half the people I knew and it was the season, so who was I to judge?

By February 2009, when Cam came out to Victoria for a week to visit me, I realized that my boyfriend, who I adored so very much, was likely not a social drinker. However, it was not until I made the decision at the end of school in March to go against all my instincts and promises to myself, and to move back to Calgary, that I fully realized the depth of his addiction. It was not until I was living in the same city as this man who made my body come alive in ways no one has ever done before, that I realized what I had gotten myself into.

I had always felt like the most important thing in Cam's life, I had grown accustomed to being first, and well I expected it. Yet suddenly it did not matter if I asked him if he could not drink one night, or asked him to leave a party with me. No, none of that mattered, and I began to feel my self-worth slipping; I watched as our relationship became more and more unhealthy. I watched and felt powerless as I became a person in that relationship who I did not want to be. I watched as I became increasingly controlling, manipulative, snarky and verbally abusive. I watched as my happy ending began to evaporate and I had to face the reality that if this was how it was only six months in, that we would likely continue to become more abusive towards each other. The hard part? Eighty percent of the time it was still amazing, we were still the best of friends and so deeply in love that there are no words to describe it.

In a way, I think Cam was my addiction. After a pregnancy scare, where I was a few days late and hadn't been consistent with birth control, I came to the realization that pregnancy was a possibility and if that were the case, I would break up with Cam. I would put this little being ahead of my own love for Cam, put it ahead of my deep need to experience the good days. So when I got my period, and I realized there was no need to leave, I was relieved at first; however, a few days later Cam once again refused to leave a friend's house and come home with me, so I left him there, went home and wrote him a letter because I knew I could never say goodbye to his face.

May 16, 2009

I'm so tired of doing this every week, I'm tired of hearing you promise it will change, that it already has changed when it hasn't. I have to write this letter because every time we try to talk you're either not interested in having the discussion, or you simply hug me and tell me everything is going to be fine, but it's not. You can't just hug this one away, Cam.

I don't understand why I didn't just go home when we got back from the bar rather than coming inside to waste another hour. I can't believe you had the nerve to ask me if you could have a beer, after you not having any more was one of the conditions of me coming in the house...as was you coming home with me. Really, you say you want me to be happy, that you love it when I smile and laugh, yet, Cam, you continuously do the one thing you know is guaranteed to make me unhappy. Yes, it is a disease, but you only acknowledge that or admit to being an alcoholic when it suits your needs, when you're drunk and trying to calm me down by excusing why you drank. So I say no, you can't drink another one, or at least that I don't want you to, but you can stay if that's what you

12

want… and true to your nature you choose to stay. You choose to stay, so you can drink more without me there monitoring your every move, so you can have some 'fun'. You knew how upset I was, you even said you have never seen me this upset before, and yet you still choose to stay and drink rather than come home with me. That's really shitty, Cam, really shitty. I don't care if you're not tired, I deserve someone who would come home because they knew I needed them. I needed you last night, but I'm happy for the reality check. I'm happy your priorities could so plainly be shown to me, even though it hurts so much.

You know for once I would love to be surprised. I would love to be put first, I would love to come before alcohol, but that's never going to happen, is it? I keep hoping for the impossible, I'm waiting for something that will never happen, or at least not in the near future. You're not ready to change, you're not ready to put anyone other than yourself first. You act like you're single half the time, you tell me it's because you're used to being single and not thinking of anyone else, and that you have to learn. Well, I'm tired of waiting for you to learn. If you act single, if you would rather have someone who doesn't nag, and would rather be able to drink when you want, as much as you want, then why don't you do that? I'm tired of doing this. If you're going to act single, you might as well be single. I know I'm emotional, but tonight was the straw that broke the camel's back; I can't do this anymore. You keep telling me I don't have it in me to break up with you; you keep saying that if I could break up with you, I would have. Well, it is partly true, but we all have our own bottom. I've reached mine.

I deserve to be happy, I deserve to be with someone who makes me happy more often than they stress me out. I have spent more time worrying, crying and being angry

in the last six months than I have in the past two years.
Yes, there have also been moments of incredible happiness
in those six months, but they get blocked out by the rest.
I deserve to be with someone who, when they know there
is something I don't like, tries to change it. Yes, you have
tried; yes, your drinking has become less often according
to you, but I'm still unhappy. I still think there is a
problem. I deserve to be with someone who would try to
do whatever they can to deal with the problem, regardless
of whether they think it is a problem or not. Why would
they do this? Because they love me and want me to be
happy even if they don't understand my reasoning and
even if it involves them making sacrifices. I know you love
me, but love is not enough, Cam. Telling me you will one
day change is not enough. Promising to provide for me in
4 years and that you will buck up when we have kids is
not enough. Do I expect you to never have a drink again?
No, not necessarily, but it's not set in stone. You keep
telling me you can stop after one or two drinks and I keep
asking you to prove it, but you can't. You make excuses
saying that you 'could' have stopped but didn't want to.
Well, once again I deserve to be with someone who,
regardless of what they want, stops and thinks "Oh,
Leanne doesn't want me to drink anymore. Shit, I want
to. Well, she's more important, so I won't." I truly don't
know what goes through your brain, how you can make
excuses to drink when you know the direct consequence is
me being upset. But I guess me being unhappy isn't a big
enough deal to actually make you think before drinking.

When we are good, we are sooo good. I can be so happy
with you, but then alcohol always comes back. I can't take
this up and down emotional shit, it is not healthy for me
in anyway, and my mental/emotional state cannot take it.
I need someone who is consistent, I need someone who I
can count on, I need someone who I can fully trust.

Alcohol ruins my ability to count on you or trust you because you are so inconsistent with what you want both from life and with us. I need someone who can plan, not the next 5 years, but at least the next week. I deserve someone who does sweet little things, that plans little things for me or us just because they want to and because they know I like that sort of thing. And don't even bring lack of money into it, because if you put all the money you spend on beer and fast food into doing things with me, we would have more than enough. I don't know Cam, I love you, I wanted to make this work, and that is why I've been trying so hard. That's why I moved back to a city I don't like, but I'm never going to change and you're never going to change, so we will never be happy, we will never work...

He begged me not to end it, but I was set at that time. I knew I needed to put me first even though it was the hardest thing I had ever done up until that point. Little did I know I would be asked to face again and again the hardest thing I had ever done, and it would only grow in difficulty as the years passed.

Over the next month we both sought refuge in the arms of others and tried to distract ourselves from the intense longing we felt, from the loss of being with your best friend. So when I got a text five weeks after having ended it, asking me to come over and hang out, I felt myself once again being drawn to Cam as if I was fully helpless to oppose. Somehow, I convinced myself that it was fine if I slept with Cam as long as we weren't dating, however, within a couple weeks of late night booty calls, Cam asked me if we could exclusively sleep together. He explained he hated the thought of me being with someone else and he didn't want to sleep with anyone else; that I was all he ever wanted, all he ever needed. So, somehow we agreed that we would not date each other or anyone else; we would have sex exclusively with each other, and at the end of the summer when I was planning to move back to Victoria, we would say goodbye. Now this might have been an okay arrangement, had we not been in love already, had we not been best friends, and had we not wanted to spend so much time together. We often looked back and laughed at ourselves, since in reality we were dating, just refusing to use the label. Everyone tried to point this out to us, but we were adamant that it was simply best friends with benefits; that it made sense because we had more fun together than we did with anyone else, so why wouldn't we hang out all the time? And why would we sleep with other random people when we had each other, who knew all the little things that made each other go wild? So people shook their heads at our refusal to acknowledge what we were and we continued on our roller coaster ride.

I wish I could tell you things were easier with his drinking and my need to control things once we were 'only' friends with benefits. But no, his drinking progressed and our fights became more and more intense. I promised myself it was done numerous times. But my love for him, my need to have him in my life was stronger than any of the pain. I was addicted to him, to the drama, to the ups and downs, especially to the ups because my God, when it was good, it was more amazing than there would ever be words to express. I knew without a shadow of a doubt that Cam wanted to change, he wanted to be healthy, he wanted to be with me and make it work. He went fishing that summer for 5 days with his dad, and during that time he would send texts or call me and discuss his revelations about how much he loved me, how much he needed me. He wanted so badly to be a father, to have children with me. I would laugh and remind him we weren't even dating and that it wasn't exactly the best timing to have kids. Cam would say he didn't care. I was his best friend and he knew I'd always be in his life and would be an amazing mother. Even if not together, he couldn't think of a better person to be the mother of his children.

"They will have your common sense, my sense of humor and both of our hazel eyes."

He would whisper this to me when we dreamt of the future. Our eyes were identical, exactly the same amount of brown, green and slight gold. Now that he is gone I sometimes will look deep into my eyes in the mirror and pretend they are his I'm looking back into, yet the twinkle is different and mine don't hold the same love his held for me.

Suddenly September was upon us and it was time for me to go back to Victoria, time for us to say goodbye. This goodbye was more gut wrenching than any of our previous ones. I remember kissing him goodbye in the driveway. I remember struggling to get air into my lungs around the sobs. I remember looking into the rearview mirror and watching Cam sink onto the pavement holding his face in his hands crying as I pulled out. I remember not knowing how I would make the drive back to Victoria, except just pushing on the gas and continuing forward. I left him with a love letter and a DVD of pictures from our time together sequenced to songs which had held relevance to us that summer.

Dear Cam,

I guess if you're reading this, it means I'm on my way back to Victoria….our summer together is over. Our summer, what a summer it has been. I think, well, at least hope that by now you know there has never been a moment I stopped loving you with my entire being. Chances are right at this moment as I drive the TransCanada highway I'm literally dying, fighting every instinct to turn around and drive back to your house and run back into your arms. Even as I type this, tears are streaming down my face because it terrifies me that the minutes are ticking away, getting closer and closer to the time I have to say goodbye. Was I strong when I hugged you that last time? I bet I can still smell you, still feel your arms around me. God, I pray never to forget the smell of you, never forget how it feels to lay in your arms, to look into your adoring eyes. Did I manage to put on my big girl smile, or did you get to see me break down and cry? You told me once that you knew that even though I looked so happy and was smiling, you knew I was dying and crying inside. You see right through me, you know me, there is no hiding anything with you...

I just called you from my mom's house because I couldn't stop crying, and needed to hear your voice, needed you to be rational for me, needed you to make me smile as no one else can. Do you remember that day? You constantly amaze me at how well you know me. I swore a long time ago that I wouldn't let anyone in, that no one would get to know me, that I would keep parts of me locked up so deep that I wouldn't even know they existed. You make me want to show those parts of me, you make me want to open the doors of my heart and take the risk that it will be broken...it has been broken, it's breaking right now, but I have no regrets, because loving you made me feel more alive than I ever have. You make me want to be a better person, you make me want to get to know myself, to love myself, to become healthy, so that I can go out in the world and touch other people's lives, that I can love again and be loved. How is it possible that you snuck past all my defenses? How did you get through all my walls? How do you know me so well? I call, I'm crying and when you ask what's wrong, when I tell you I'm crying because of 'us', you laugh in the way only you can and state that you already know that. You go on to describe how you can picture me sitting at my mom's writing you this letter, listening to Within Temptation and that the only thing that is missing is the glass of wine... We then laugh about how I've got my water bottle instead of the wine. Yep that's me, you know me inside out, maybe I'm not as complicated as I thought I was, or maybe that's what love is all about, letting the other person in.

I feel safe to be me. Even when I try not to be me you see through it, you know me, and you know the best part about that? You love me in spite of really seeing me. I've always thought I was unlovable, always thought I had to be extra good to have people like me. You have helped me love myself, you have shown me that I deserve to be loved for me just as I am, all my quirks and annoying habits included, because they are a part of me and make me who I am. Cam, I hope you know you deserve the same kind of love. You are one of the most incredible people I have ever been blessed to have in my life and I love you with my entire being. I love you as the person you show the world, the goofy, funny, guy who makes me laugh even when I'm spitting mad, the only person who has been able to get me out of 'a mood' with a hug and a quick couple words. But I also love the other side of you that most people don't get to see, the side which is gentle, loving, likes to stand outside on the porch wrapped in a blanket and watch the trees blow in the wind, the sensitive side of you.

I love you for everything you are and I love you for everything I know you have the potential to grow into. When I look at you, I do not only see you as you are at this moment, I see who you truly are as a person and who you are becoming or will become if you continue doing the work. I'm so proud of you, Cam, so very proud. Yes, there have been moments of great disappointment, moments I thought my heart could not take one more second of pain, moments I didn't know how to put one foot in front of the other, but through it all I loved you, and that's why it hurt so much. You asked me once why I couldn't just accept you as you were, why I was trying to change you. I'm sorry I ever made you feel you weren't good enough for me. The truth is I could not stand watching you hurt yourself, you were not being good enough for yourself. I know you deserve better than you are giving yourself and I cannot sit back and watch you slowly destroy yourself, because that hurts me more than walking away. But walking away has proved much harder than I thought possible.

I believe in you. I believe the person I see when I look at you is coming into being, and I am extremely excited for you because, well, the world is at your fingertips. We have so many memories…so many emotions flood to the surface when I think of you, when I remember the feel of your touch, the sound of your laugh, the way you would look at me. You make me feel safe, you make me feel special, as if everything is exactly as it should be and nothing else matters when it is just us. I wish it was always so simple, I wish that nothing else matter, I wish it could just be us forever. I'm falling apart right now and questioning how it is possible that I can love someone so much and yet not be able to be with them. How is that fair? Even our summer, what was supposed to be a crazy in love summer, was spent mostly broken up, mostly longing to have it work but knowing it wouldn't. My heart and head have fought constantly over you and whether love is enough, it has literally driven me crazy. I've tried to move on, but couldn't. I can't imagine my life without you, the thought of it terrifies me, leaves me feeling sick to my stomach. I will love you forever, there will never be a day you do not reside in my heart, I'll take you everywhere I go, and cherish our memories…forever.

As hard as I cry as I type this, I know it is time for us to let go, to try to move on, to love others and open our hearts to try again, because we both deserve to find true happiness. I wish that happiness could have been with each other, really I do; part of me refuses to believe that we won't end up together in time; refuses to believe that we won't have beautiful children with the most intense hazel eyes, your common sense and my kindness; refuses to believe that happy ever after will not be ours together, but we can't wait for that day. Remember me, remember how much I loved you and that I always wanted what was best for you, would have done anything to make you happy. Remember you deserve to be loved fully for who you are. Don't settle for anything less, don't settle for someone who doesn't push you to be the best you can be, don't settle for someone who doesn't make you laugh, who isn't afraid to be a huge goof (yes, we did reclaim it), who won't go to any length to make you smile. Remember you make me smile...Remember you make me laugh and remember you are cute, remember the sound of my voice as I tell you for the 40th time how very cute you are and that I love you as I lean in to kiss your arm...Remember my weird little quirks because I'll never forget yours.

Life may be taking us in separate directions, but you have changed my life, you have left an imprint on my heart that will never fade away. Thank you for loving me. I wish loving you was all that mattered, I wish you loving me was all that mattered, I wish love was enough, because if it was we would be so happy, we would have everything anyone could ever wish for. Love only... That was what I said and wanted so badly to believe, but life is more complicated than that, we need more than love only. That part was easy, love came so easily, it is the rest that we struggled with. For today, I feel as if my heart has been shredded but I know we will be okay, we will laugh and smile again, we will love again, and until that day we will just be a phone call away. You never will be just a memory to me, Cam, you will always be the one that got away...but then again life doesn't always make sense.

Goodbye Cam, I love you...

We had agreed that our exclusive sleeping together arrangement made no sense living in different provinces, so we were essentially free to see who we wanted and to do what we pleased with them. But the heart doesn't listen so easily and we talked for hours every day. Both of us started dating, but would call immediately after a date to tell the horror stories and laugh together about how horrible the dating pool was. Cam asked his mom to pay for my flight back to Calgary for Thanksgiving, and we spent 5 days wrapped in each other's arms, only to pull apart with even more pain than before. By Christmas I realized that nothing was changing, I realized that Cam was not going to quit drinking, that I was never going to move on when completely in love with him and still talking to him every day, and that we would never have a healthy relationship if things continued in this manner. Hardest of all, I realized that we could never just be friends, that we were far too attracted to each other and completely in love to ever just be friends again. And thus I came to the realization that we needed to say goodbye for good. We needed to realize that we no longer could have contact.

Anyone who has had to walk away from a relationship that they still desperately wanted to be in will understand the void that fills your heart on the days when you wake up and do not see a text from them, when you go to sleep and realize you didn't have any contact with them. I tried to stay busy, tried not to go crazy wondering what he was doing or with whom. I spent more time crying than I thought was possible. And then I met someone. He was wonderful and he thought the world of me, yet I couldn't fully give myself to him, because I was still in love with Cam, even if we weren't talking. But he was a good distraction. I had a trip planned to Calgary for April to see my mom and actually contemplated cancelling it because I didn't trust myself to go and not see Cam, to not be pulled back in. I was still in contact with Cam's mom and sister, and we were all going to do dinner together. I thought this could be a safe place to see Cam as other people would be around and we couldn't let our attraction get the better of us.

Before we had stopped talking, Cam had asked me to sew him a quilt for his bed and I had been working on it for a couple of months. I finished it when we were no longer talking and decided to bring it to Calgary and give it to him as a final goodbye present. For me, it was a way that I would know he would always have something to remind him of me, something to remind him of how much I loved him, even if I couldn't be in his life. This was very important to me and I spent hours designing and sewing the king size quilt with a fleece back. So, in April 2010 when I got together with Cam, his mom and his sister, I gave him the quilt and a poem I wrote to go along with it as a token of my love, as a final wish, an intended final goodbye.

I don't know how life will turn out. It seems just when I think I have it figured out things change, so as much as I hope you are always a part of my life, I recognize you may not be. Regardless of what happens, I hope this blanket will serve as a reminder of our time together, of our friendship, of the laughs, the tears, of how hard we tried to make it work, of the sour taste and sadness I believe we both felt when it didn't. Let this blanket be a reminder of our love, of how much I adored you, because the hours I spent picking out fabric, ironing it, cutting and sewing it all together were filled with loving thoughts and wishes for you and your future, even if I am no longer a part of that future. That is why it was and is so important to me that you have the quilt. I will never forget what we had, how beautiful and yet dysfunctional we were. I have never fallen so hard or fast for another person; it was a whirlwind of intensity.

One of the squares has Inukshuks on it. I chose to place the Inukshuk square in the upper left hand corner of the quilt so it will cover and guard your heart... Yeah I know, I'm a geek. The Inukshuk is traditionally a rock formation used by the Inuit People to lead each other home. Cam, you became my home, my everything. You led me home, you led me back to you countless times, even though we were separated by thousands of miles. You were my Inukshuk, my way home. May you find your way home wherever that may be, whomever that may be with. We may go in different directions, but I hope the Inukshuk will help guide your path, will remind you of your past, our past, of where you come from as you set out on your journey. And maybe one day it will lead you back to me…but maybe not and I guess I will have to be okay with that. Although the entire blanket is my gift to you, that one square is my signature of love, is the summary of hopes and dreams I have for you, is my private message to you that I will always hold you in my heart. You will always be a part of me. That square is my promise to you that I will never forget you or stop believing in you. That square is our square; a dedication to all we went through, a tribute to our love which no one, not even us, can fully understand.

Forever in my heart,

Lee Lee

Cam read the poem, got up and threw it in the garbage, turned to me and said in a confused angry voice, "It sounds like you're still in love with me." And I answered the only way I knew, truthfully, that I was. We hung out a few times. He hated that I was dating someone, but I maintained that we had tried and it hadn't worked, that love was simply not enough.

Yet on April 17, 2010 Cam sat down on the couch next to me and started to cry. He looked at me as tears streamed down his face; between his sobs he told me that he had lived for the last few months without me in his life and he didn't want to live another day without me being a part of it. He told me that during that time he had tried to pretend he didn't miss me as much as he did, but having me back these last few days had reminded him of all that had been missing and he couldn't imagine going back to life without me. As he cried he asked me what it would take to get me back, begging me not to tell him he didn't have another chance.

I told him that we would need to do couple's counselling, and he would need to quit drinking forever; that if he ever had another drink again, I expected him to do AA, something I knew he desperately did not want to do for whatever reason. He agreed and promised that this time he was serious, thanking me for another chance. I knew it was the riskiest and most illogical choice I could have made, to leave a good stable relationship in order to go back to one that had been havoc and heartbreaking historically. Although I had heard his promises more times than I can count, somehow I knew this time was different. Why would someone do this? I knew that if I followed my head and told him no, enough was enough and I couldn't do it again, if I said goodbye and walked away, I would always wonder if he would have followed through, would have wondered what could have been if I just believed, and I knew I couldn't live with that.

So I said yes. I agreed to embark on a life of sobriety with him, to stand in solidarity with him and our new way of life. It will forever remain a decision I am grateful I made, it will remain one of the best choices I have ever made, even if ultimately it resulted in more pain then I could have ever imagined and, in the end, still left me without him. My heart had gotten me in trouble many times before, but this time I am still forever grateful I listened to it rather than my head that day.

Chapter Three:
A New Life, A New Chance, A Short Forever

We quickly learned that not all of our problems had their roots in drinking. However, our ability to remain rational and understand the other's point of view was greatly increased by our choice to live in sobriety. Our fights took on an adult dimension, and we knew that no matter what the disagreement or struggle, our relationship and love for each other outweighed it. With the help of a few different counsellors, we learned ways to appropriately show love and ask for our needs to be met. Doing this all from two provinces continued to present challenges for us, and so in August 2011 Cam moved to Victoria to be with me. But I'm getting ahead of myself.

A couple months after we decided to give this rollercoaster ride another go, I bought a condo in Victoria and Cam rented a U-Haul to move my furniture from storage in Calgary down to Victoria for me. Two days after we moved my stuff in, we were coming home at 11 one night after driving for over an hour. I really had to pee and when I say that, I mean I REALLY had to pee! I mentioned that I might pee in the parkade but Cam told me I was being ridiculous and could wait the four floors to get to my condo. By about floor two Cam started making jokes of some sort. Really, he was just being his normal everyday hilarious self, but on this particular day I had a very full bladder. And suddenly I realized I couldn't hold it any longer; in fact, I was peeing all over the elevator floor and couldn't stop.

Cam looked back and forth, between me and the floor that was becoming increasingly wet, with horror. By the time we reached the fourth floor I had managed to stop the endless flow of urine and we were standing in about an inch of pee. If this wasn't humiliating enough on its own, when the elevator doors opened, naturally another young couple stood there waiting to go down.

The girl screamed as Cam and I quickly pushed past them and ran down the hall to the safety of my condo. Why do I tell this story other than to embarrass myself further and give you something to laugh at? I tell it because it is one of the thousand stories I have that illustrates how amazing Cam was, how kind, thoughtful, and down to earth he was. As soon as we got into the condo, he told me to go shower and that he was going to go clean up the pee. He proceeded to take towels, paper towels and vinegar out to the elevator and spent the next thirty minutes cleaning that elevator so that no one else would know what had happened there. He then came back, took my urine sodden clothes and towels, and put a load of laundry on before coming and giving me a hug and telling me how much he loved me.

No, I'm not making that part up. Trust me, the next day he couldn't stop laughing and thought it was the funniest thing he had ever seen. But that night when I was so ashamed that I could hardly look at him and didn't know how I could live in the same building as the couple that saw us, he just held me and told me that everyone pees their pants at times. He went on to tell me stories about him pooing his pants as an adult when a fart turned out to be more than he bargained for. He did everything to normalize what had happened and to reassure me it was okay, nothing to be embarrassed about. And he succeeded in the way only Cam could.

Why? Because I trusted him more than I did anyone else in the entire world. This further set the ground for our complete and utter acceptance of each other. When I told friends how we were, they would shake their heads and say we were weird, that they wouldn't want that level of intimacy with their partners. But for us there was no other way to be; it was all in.

When we got back together it was with the full understanding that we wanted it to be forever, that we wanted to spend the rest of our lives together. The funny thing is that, when people think that or say that sort of thing, one person is almost always guaranteed to be left alone at some point. We say 'the rest of our lives', but one often dies before the other, and one is left to fend with life on their own. However, in 2010 at the ages of 25 and 26, our inevitable death was far from our minds. We started talking about getting married. We started planning our future. For the first time, with our relationship becoming increasingly healthy and with Cam sticking to his sobriety promise, suddenly it felt safe to dream.

Now in case I haven't mentioned it yet, I'm a HUGE control freak! And I had some very specific ideas about what it would look like to get engaged. We would be watching a movie when visiting each other, and I would exclaim, "Oh God, never ask me like that." I didn't want it in front of people, not with family or friends present, nothing embarrassing, nothing corny, and it had to be romantic. Cam handled it well, but there were a few times he got frustrated with me and told me he was very stressed about how to ask me, and feared that he would mess up somehow.

Before asking me to marry him, Cam called my mom; he apologized for how he had treated me historically, promised to continue getting healthier, promised to continue loving me more and more each day, and asked for her blessing. She cried along with him and welcomed him to the family, for she knew he meant everything he said, she knew he loved me with every ounce of his body and made me happier than I could have ever hoped to be. Cam couldn't keep a secret from me for the life of him, and so I knew the day he bought the engagement ring as I got a text while in class in Victoria stating, "*I made a very big important purchase today ;-).*" I didn't pry because I didn't want to know, but two months later when I was coming home for Christmas, I started to put limits down, not only around how to ask me, but certain dates he had to avoid.

Our dating anniversary was December 11th so that was naturally when I was expecting him to ask; however, we were doing an early Christmas with my family on the 10th and so I told him he had to ask me by then so I could tell them all in person that night. The catch? I was flying in to Calgary on December 3rd, so essentially he had a one week window to ask me and keep to my parameters for how to ask. He made it perfect.

Cam picked me up at the airport with flowers on December 3, 2010 and we hugged and kissed, excited to get two weeks together after three months apart. Just like a gentleman, he carried my two suitcases back to the truck and we stood beside his truck in the airport parking lot, where we had exchanged so many I love yous, where we had held each other and cried before parting, and where we had jumped around clinging to each other because it had hurt to be apart.

We stood there and he asked me to grab his keys from his coat pocket. I reached in and immediately stopped mid-sentence, and looked at him. I felt the box, the box that somehow every girly-girl knows the feeling of, even if she has never touched one before. I started stuttering, "Are you sure? Right now? Are you sure?" I was sure he had forgotten it was in there and had made a mistake asking me to grab the keys. Cam had the biggest smile on his face as he watched me flounder and managed to say, "Yes, take it out silly."

And so, I pulled the box out and opened it up. With tears in my eyes I looked up into his, which radiated more love than I could ever explain. We stood there a moment until I said, "Well, are you going to ask me?" And Cam, putting my suitcases down, took the ring out and asked, "Baby, will you marry me?" He placed it on my hand as I whispered yes and threw my arms around him. It was the perfect engagement, at the place that had started it all, the one place that held all our happy squeals and saddest tears. It was private, with no one in any of the cars nearby. It was ours, all ours.

That night we went to Montana's BBQ & Bar for dinner and then went to watch the movie Tangled in the theatre because, well, that's us; kids at heart. We were more in love and happier than I could have ever hoped for, it felt like life was just beginning, like our dreams were finally starting to come true, like life was finally starting to work out.

Chapter Four:
Rewind To Me

Loving and losing Cam were not my first experiences with struggle and they were not the first obstacles I faced in my short life, however they were the most all-encompassing. I was born in Regina, Saskatchewan on May 3, 1984 as the first, and as time would have it, only child to my parents.

Shortly after my second birthday my parents decided to embark on an adventure and move to the Land of the Midnight Sun. My father was a family physician and opened a practice in Dawson City, Yukon, which my mother helped him run while also raising me. There is something magical about growing up in a small, isolated community, especially during the harsh winter months of near complete darkness and stretches of -50 degrees Celsius. People learn to rely on each other and form community in ways I have not witnessed in urban centers. It is not simply about connection; rather, it is about survival.

Survival emotionally as people come to rely on each other to break the monotony of day in and day out snow, cold and seemingly never-ending darkness. Survival physically as the luxury of calling a tow truck or repair person when something breaks does not always exist and could mean the difference between life and death.

I loved growing up in the Yukon; loved the warm sun that never seemed to set all summer, being able to walk as far as my little legs would carry me in the wilderness with only my parents and wildlife for company, going on Ski-Doo rides or, better yet, being pulled on a sled behind one while giggling out of pure excitement mixed with just the right amount of fear. It was with devastation that I learned we would be leaving my home to move to Calgary, Alberta when I was 10 years old. However, it is a move that changed the course of my life and opened doors that simply were not available in the Yukon.

I was diagnosed with a learning disability when I was seven years old and began to receive some extra help at school, as well as having a tutor at home. By the time I was nine years old it had become apparent that rather than improving, my grades were continuing to suffer and, indeed, my reading and spelling levels were not progressing, regardless of the effort put forth. After much research my parents decided we would move to Calgary, Alberta so that I could be enrolled in Foothills Academy, a school for children with learning disabilities. Although at the time this was not something I was agreeable to, it did not take long for me to realize this was in my best interest. Within two years of attending Foothills Academy, my reading level went from grade one to grade twelve. The alternative ways they taught somehow worked for me and something just "clicked" inside my brain.

While I likely could have re-integrated into the public system due to my grades consistently being in the high 80's - 90's through Junior High School and High School, I decided to graduate from Foothills Academy rather than risk falling behind or being overwhelmed in the public system. As an adult reflecting on the many ways life can turn out differently based on single decisions we make, I am very appreciative of my parents ignoring my pleas not to take me from my home and everything that was familiar to me and their decision to move me to Calgary.

For had it not been for this decision, there is a very huge likelihood I would not have graduated High School. Indeed, even if I had the probability of going on to get my Undergrad as well as Masters of Social Work, which has allowed me to work as a Family Counsellor, it would have been extremely unlikely given the degree of which I struggled with my schooling prior to Foothills Academy. And, of course, had it not been for the move to Calgary, I never would have had the opportunity to meet Cam.

Shortly after moving to Calgary, my parents decided to get a divorce and my dad moved back to the Yukon to continue running his medical practice. While the divorce was difficult for me as a 12 year old, it also was not a surprise due to my parents not having gotten along for a number of years, and in that way it was a bit of a relief. I continued to return to the Yukon to visit my dad and old friends whenever I wasn't in school until Cam and I began dating in 2008. When I was 16 years old my dad and stepmom, whom he met through work and began to date a few years earlier, blessed me with a little brother. He quickly became my world as I had always longed to be a big sister. This blessing was tripled when my sisters were born during my 18th and 21st years. While I am technically old enough to be a parent to all of them and thus this not being a standard sibling relationship, I have adored watching them grow and playing big sister. They were my guardian angels reminding me I had a reason to keep going during a very tumultuous time in my life.

My parents had named me Elizabeth Leanne; however, from the time I was born I went by my middle name. After graduating high school, I decided to change the name I went by to my first name. It is for this reason that Cam always called me Leanne. Indeed, anyone who knew me before I turned 18 has continued to call me Leanne. I will forever have two names I go by. I made the change because I wanted to escape who I was, start over and recreate my identity when I went to University. Unfortunately, changing who we are and learning to truly love who we currently are is not accomplished in one simple task, such as changing one's name.

When I was 13 years old, I was diagnosed with Generalized Anxiety Disorder and Major Depression. I was prescribed Zoloft to deal with both, which I took for a number of years before deciding it was not helping as we had hoped. Looking back and based on the recounts of my parents, it is quite possible that the disposition towards anxiety started when I was only a small child. My teenage years and early 20's were filled with insecurities around who I was, how I fit in the world as well as if I was good enough or worthy. While that may not sound unlike the average teenager, this resulted in a disconnect with myself, which then turned to self-hatred. In an attempt to self-regulate my wildly out of control emotions I engaged in self-harm, in the form of cutting, on a regular basis.

At times I felt numb and like I was simply floating through life; however, when the blade would cut through my skin suddenly, I was reminded that I was alive, that I could indeed feel something. I realize it's next to impossible to understand if you have never engaged in self-harm, how hurting yourself could indeed offer solace, but it does and for years it was my secret survival weapon. During this time, I also rivalled with suicidal thoughts and the desire to escape this world. With the arrival of each of my siblings the intensity of self-loathing seemed to dissipate for a period of time and be replaced by wonder at this new little life. Instead of focusing on my own pain, I focused on all the little changes they were undergoing. However, these reprieves were always short lived and I would be dragged back into the darkness of self-destruction.

At age 19, a psychiatrist diagnosed me with Bipolar Disorder, which felt both like a straight-jacket and as if someone had lifted the curtain. It is not a diagnosis anyone wants to hear applied to them, but after years of never knowing which version of myself I would wake up to and self-hatred, it was strangely validating to understand what was going on.

I worked with various therapists to learn new ways to regulate my emotions and learn to forgive myself for my previously destructive ways. Through counselling, I came up with safety plans to manage the hounding suicidal thoughts, as well as discovering that regulation of my diet, in particular sugar and caffeine consumption, along with as regular exercise and adhering to a strict sleep hygiene routine, I was able to smooth out the intensity of the highs and lows.

In early February 2008, I received my first shipment of True Hope EMPowerplus, a multivitamin that had been designed specifically to help those diagnosed with Bipolar Disorder regulate their emotions. At that time, I do not believe there had been any double-blind studies; however, I was willing to give anything natural a try and had read some very convincing testimonials. Within three days of starting to take the multivitamin supplement I too became one of those testimonials, as it was the first time in years that all thoughts of suicide or self-harm seemed to simply disappear. Initially, I expected them to return and explained the sudden shift in my disposition as a placebo effect.

As weeks turned into months, I began to become more confident and excited that quite possibly this new relaxed and stable version of me could be here to stay. However, it was not until I tried to lower the number of vitamins a day I was taking with the assistance of True Hope support people, I felt a return of some of the manic symptoms, in particular the inability to sleep. I now truly believed that somehow this vitamin was allowing my brain to function in ways it had never been able to on its own.

As the years passed, I continued to dutifully take EMPowerplus in accordance to True Hopes instructions as they altered and improved the supplement. To me, the greatest testimony to the strength and legitimacy of this wonderful supplement was that throughout the time that Cam was sick as well as during the agony of losing him I did not experience a return of any Bipolar symptoms. Yes, I had a deep desire to no longer be alive and desperately wanted to join him, but this desire was based on the reality that I had just lost my love, whereas my previously suicidal thoughts had been based on a desire to escape myself and the seemingly never ending pain within myself. It may be hard to see them as separate, yet the difference is strikingly clear to me.

Cam and Elizabeth (aka Leanne) in Junior High School

Cam the night he let us girls do his make up
and dress him up while in Junior High.

December 2008 when Cam and Elizabeth
first reconnected with each other and started falling in love.

December 2008 the goofiness is real, the bond unbreakable.

In Victoria, British Columbia in February 2009
when Cam came to visit Elizabeth for a week.

Victoria February 2009 visit

Cam and Elizabeth Victoria 2009 visit

August 2009 on a camping trip we did from
Calgary, Alberta through Kelowna, British Columbia.
Picture from slideshow Elizabeth made Cam

August 2009 camping trip which was also in the slideshow

The quilt Elizabeth sewed Cam as a "goodbye" gift in April 2010

The Inukshuk square Elizabeth references in the goodbye
poem/note she wrote Cam
in April 2010 just before he stopped drinking.

December 3, 2010 Cam and Elizabeth got engaged!

Going out to celebrate the engagement
and two years of being in each other's lives, Dec. 11, 2010

Engagement photo shoot July 7, 2012
days before going to Victoria to pack up the condo

Chapter Five:
Life Changes With One Word

Cam had moved to Victoria in the fall of 2011, but it became clear within months that financially we couldn't live the life we wanted there. So, it was decided we would move back to Calgary. Cam moved back to Calgary and I finished my Masters of Social Work on-campus courses at the University of Victoria, before putting my condo up for sale, staging it for viewing and then joining him in Calgary with our new dog, Bentley. Finally it sold and we arranged to drive back to Victoria, pack it up and begin looking for a permanent home in Calgary. Given my dislike for Calgary, this was a big decision. But I loved Cam more than I disliked Calgary, so for me it was worth it.

I remember going for a walk on my own with our dog, right before we were going to drive to Victoria, BC to pack up my little condo. I had this sudden and very happy realization that many of my dreams were all coming true in the perfect order. I was one of those girls that people would roll their eyes at with jealousy, because I was hitting my milestones on the head perfectly.

Now of course, I knew how hard I had worked and that none of these 'milestones' were particularly easy nor were they handed to me, but if I was to tell a perfect stranger about my current life, it sounded amazing. I had everything I wanted in that moment and knew that there was no reason to really fear that the rest of my dreams, the rest of Cam's and my dreams, wouldn't come true. I was 28, nearly done my Masters of Social Work degree, engaged to be married in a year to my best friend, had a dog whom we both adored, had just sold my condo in Victoria and had been emailing with a realtor in Calgary. Life was turning out better than I had ever possibly dreamed of or hoped for. I was so unbelievably happy.

And I knew exactly how the next few years would play out. We would buy a house that fall, I would finish my Masters by 2013 and get a job, we would get married in June 2013 and get pregnant in 2014 or 2015, depending on where both our careers were.

We had agreed there was no rush to get married after our engagement because we already knew we would spend the rest of our lives together, regardless of whether we were married. Similarly, we saw no rush to have children as we had all our lives ahead of us and a good few years before my biological clock started clicking. What I wouldn't do to go back to that moment! What I wouldn't give to feel so secure and safe in the absolute knowledge that everything is happening perfectly, and as it should be, and sure that my future would be nothing but a story-book ending.

On July 11, 2012 we packed up what little furniture remained in my condo and moved it into U-Haul storage. On that day, Cam noticed a lump on the right side of his neck, almost like his lymph node was really enflamed. I vividly remember dismissing it as nothing to be concerned about, as only a of couple months before a very similar lump had shown up in the same spot and by the time Cam was able to get in to see his doctor, it had gone. I figured that similarly this one would be gone in a couple days. Over the last number of months, Cam had been struggling with pain in his ribs and hips.

Initially in November 2011, we thought he had pulled a muscle in Pilates when he woke up one day with intense pain in his rib. After a couple of weeks it dissipated only to return but on the other side. Again, we dismissed this with the assumption he had been overcompensating when hurting and had accidently strained the other side. Some days the pain was gone, others a mild ache and some so bad Cam had tears in his eyes and struggled with breathing.

In February 2012, he returned to Calgary with the plan for me to follow once able. He began going to the doctor regarding the unexplainable pain he was having; however, Cam was simply prescribed muscle relaxants and pain medications which did not help. That spring the pain moved to his hips with a similar presentation of changing intensity of pain. Some days he struggled to walk from the pain and on other days we would go for long hikes with little difficulty. Between February and July, Cam went to his family doctor 8 times. Sadly, his mysterious pain was not seen to warrant further investigation.

On July 12th Cam drove up island to Ucluelet to meet his dad for a fishing trip, and I went to stay with one of my girlfriends in Victoria. I didn't even think about that little lump that was just a bit smaller than a golf ball. July 17th couldn't come soon enough, as both of us knew that these few days apart were going to be the last time we would sleep in separate beds. We were really starting our life together and both of us were beside ourselves with excitement. When Cam came and picked me up from my girlfriend's home, I immediately commented on the lump on the side of his neck. It had grown to the size of a baseball in only 5 days. At my insistence, Cam called his family doctor back in Calgary and managed to set an appointment for the afternoon of July 20th. With the appointment booked, neither of us thought anymore about it and just started looking forward to the future.

We loaded the U-Haul trailer again and managed to just barely catch the last ferry over to Vancouver. Everything about that night was magical. I have played it over in my mind thousands of times. It was late, but we played a game of Frisbee with Bentley on the car deck, and laughed during the entire ferry ride. On the way out to Victoria, we had camped at Shuswap Lake so we could go swimming and roast hot dogs, and we had planned to camp there again on the way back. We had even booked a campsite for the night of the 17th. Being apart for a few days, paired with the excitement of finally getting to start our lives together, it drove Cam to beg and finally convince me to trash the camping idea and get a hotel room where we could have a little more room and privacy to do as we pleased.

I have never regretted that decision, as that was possibly one of the most passionate nights in our relationship. I have thought of that night on many occasions, and wondered if somehow unconsciously we knew that in a few days everything was going to change, that the security we felt and the promise of the future would be shattered. We had had great sex before and Cam always argued that we had even better sex afterwards, but that night held a different level of passion, a different air of desire and desperation. It also held only promise, no fear, no sadness, and no question that one day he might not be there to have sex with. There was no need for any of those thoughts and so we both just gave into pure desire and longing for the other.

Cam and I both loved driving; we particularly loved driving with each other. We often marveled at the quality of conversations we would have, and how we could sort out any problem if stuck in a car with each other. We designed our dream house and wrote down all the things we wanted in it, and that were important to us, on little bits of scrap paper, all while driving.

Much of our relationship had been dealt with either over the phone, while driving (it wasn't illegal back then), or while we were stuck inside those four little walls. So, a 10-hour drive with the love of my life, who could make me laugh even if I was in a mad mood, was inevitably wonderful. I remember, and will forever cherish, Cam looking at me as we passed Banff Townsite and him telling me that he had had a wonderful time on this trip with me, and how much he loved me. I hold onto the feeling of knowing I was someone's everything, that the person I adored most in the world felt the same about me. That all we needed was each other for the world to be complete.

On the 18th we stayed in a little motel in Revelstoke, BC and took Bentley for a walk along the river where he swam after sticks we threw in for him. It was gorgeously hot out, and we felt no need to be anywhere but exactly where we were. That night we went out to an amazing restaurant with only two other people there the entire time. We arrived in Calgary late the night of the 19th and just crashed at his mom's house, happy and ready to start the next part of our journey. We did not yet realize what the next part would entail.

After unloading the U-Haul, we drove to his doctor's appointment on July 20th. I still can feel the sink of my stomach when he came out and said he needed to go to emergency; that his doctor had instructed him to go there. What I can't remember is why I didn't go with him. I know that his mom ended up taking him and that he stayed overnight. But I have no idea why I didn't go. Part of me thinks that we just didn't want to think it was anything serious, and part of me just wasn't ready to enter that world quite yet. The rest of the days blend into each other. Cam met with an infectious disease specialist the next morning to rule that out as a possibility, and then came home.

We were so eager to start the next phase of our life, that even with the growing concern of what was going on, we met up with our realtor to go look at homes. We simply would not accept that things were not as perfect as we had thought. On July 22nd I went to look at more homes Cam and I had picked out, while he went to have a biopsy done on his neck. The plan was for him to meet the realtor and me afterwards, to continue looking. I got the call as we were looking at the first house. Cam's voice was controlled, but in a way that I could tell he was fighting to control it. He said that I needed to come to the hospital right now; that they thought it was cancer.

Somehow, I calmly asked the realtor to drive me back to Cam's mom's house and apologized for having to cancel on him. On the way to the hospital, I called the girlfriend I had stayed with only days before in Victoria and cried and cried. I still remember her telling me that it was all going to work out alright, and thinking that she had to be right, how could anything other than it being okay happen? On July 22, 2012 my life changed forever, even if I did not realize it at that time. Although, when I think back on that day, I did know and I cried for the devastation of it then, and for what I knew was to come.

The doctors explained to Cam and me where all the cancer was. They explained that there were two tumors in his heart, the large one in his neck, and that there were lytic lesions throughout his ribs, spine, hips, jaw bone, and shoulders. The belief was that the cancer started in his heart, and with every pump sent cancer cells throughout his body. We laid in each other's arms that night in the hospital bed and just cried, sobbed, and tried to keep oxygen in our lungs. Neither of us slept more than a couple hours, I remember feeling too devastated to sleep, and not wanting to waste one second with him.

The nurses were so good to me and brought in a little cot on the second night so that I could sleep in the room with him, but not in the same tiny bed. There were so many different doctors and nurses, tests to be run and explanations that I struggled to understand; words, which meant nothing to me at the time, but quickly became a standard part of my vocabulary.

One of these doctors explained that the chemotherapy that Cam would likely be on would result in him being infertile. Never had I longed to have a baby as badly as I did in that moment, and the months that came after. I had never questioned that we would have children. It had been something we had discussed from the time we were only dating. You may remember that Cam would tease me that they would have his sense of humor, my smart brains and both of our beautiful hazel eyes. No, there never was a question of whether we would have kids; just how many and whether it was best to have a boy or girl first.

But just as one cannot control whether they have a boy or girl first, we could not have predicted that this 'given' was anything but. I called the fertility clinic and we were scheduled to come down so that Cam could leave a sample of his semen. It all felt like it was largely out of a movie, and I'm happy and amazed that we were able to find the entire situation so entertaining. I think we were both just so relieved that there was this option; true, it was not how we had planned on having children and would end up costing a lot more money than had been planned, but we still had an option. There was a lot of hope for the future that we were being proactive and ensuring that cancer would not take away our dream of being parents. It was explained to us that no other fluids could be included in the sample, thus no lubricants, saliva or vaginal fluids could be on the penis at time of ejaculation. So I went into the back room as more of a moral support rather than actual assistant. Oh, how we laughed as we stood in the room, with a pile of magazines Cam was scared to touch due to how many other hands with a specific purpose had touched them. Similarly, he did not want to put a movie on and so he simply settled for looking up porn on his phone while standing, with me holding the container. And that was how our potential future children came to live in a plastic container and eventually moved into 13 straws, frozen in the fertility clinic.

Now to be honest, this was not an easy thing to accept. We were still raw from learning about the cancer only days before, and now we were faced with the reality that even if he got better, having children was not going to be how we had always envisioned it. For myself, I had spent years ensuring I didn't get pregnant, and now this dream of mine was no longer so easily obtainable. Cam and I had discussed getting pregnant for the last two years but I had wanted to wait until I was finished my Master's degree and we were married. I just didn't see the rush.

Now I questioned this decision. My plan had been to have my IUD removed when Cam and I were ready, but not tell him exactly when and to give it to him in a jewelry box with a little note. Yes, kind of strange, but I knew he would be thrilled and likely drag me into the bedroom with a whole new purpose to sex. And for Cam, well, he struggled with feeling like he was losing a part of his identity, that he was somehow less manly because he was infertile. It affected his self-esteem in ways no one other than myself and maybe our counsellor knew.

We were both so grateful there was even the option of doing in-vitro fertilization, but it was a shock that something we had thought of as being a special magical and fun time was going to be turned into an invasive, expensive medical procedure. We tried to remind ourselves that the end result was the same, and that when we held our baby for the first time it wouldn't matter how they came into being, we would just be so happy.

In early August we learned that Cam had high grade spindle cell sarcoma, a very rare form of cancer. It was explained that while quite treatable in its early stage, once it has metastasized, which Cam's had, only 50% of people survive a year. Hearing this was like having the oxygen sucked out of our lungs. I remember neither of us cried in the hospital room; we listened and I asked questions, took pamphlets and wrote down everything they said. I realized that I needed to stay fully present in those meetings, and that I needed to ask the hard questions no one else wanted to hear the answers to; that while in that room I could hold Cam's hand, but I had to remove myself from being his wife if I was going to serve as a support to him outside of those walls. I realized that we were facing the largest struggle either of us had ever known, and that I had to gain as much knowledge about what we were facing as I could, and that I couldn't allow my emotions to stifle that.

As we walked back to the car, I had to jog to keep up with Cam's pace, and finally caught him and pulled him into my arms, where we both just let ourselves feel the fear in its horrifying rawness. Somehow we got home that day and both started making phone calls, rallying our troops of friends and family who would support us to differing degrees throughout this journey.

With the realization that time might not be on our side, I became obsessed with doing my own research. I was determined to find a way to cure Cam no matter where in the world it required us to go. Initially, I was looking at cancer centers throughout the world that treated sarcoma, as well as recording in my new medical journal the forms of chemo and radiation that were standardly used to treat spindle cell sarcoma. I would write down all my questions, and anything I did research on and wanted to ensure the doctors at the Tom Baker Cancer Centre in Calgary were aware of. When we would meet with Cam's oncologist, she would answer my questions and respond to my findings. I was happy to hear that the standard treatments in the expensive centers in the states were the same as was being offered here. We agreed to do it their way, and to listen to what the doctors said, even though it went against all our logic.

We both took lots of different vitamins and tried to eat foods that contained antioxidants. Then suddenly all of this was no longer allowed for him, due to the potential that antioxidants could interfere with chemo. I read the pamphlets and books about living with cancer and being a caregiver within a few days, highlighting the parts that were of particular interest to me so that I could return to them. My focus and drive for life became understanding everything I could about cancer, about sarcoma, and about what possible treatments existed.

On August 22nd, one month after our world had been turned upside down, I decided at 4 in the morning that cancer was not going to destroy all my dreams. I had met a girlfriend for coffee the night before and had been talking/crying about our planned wedding, which was 10 months away. I was faced with the realization that there was a large likelihood, based on statistics, that Cam would not be alive at that time; that our wedding would never be a reality. I knew I wanted to marry him. I wanted nothing more than the privilege of calling him my husband. I wanted that for the rest of MY life and had hoped it would be a good 50 years before facing saying goodbye. But I was realistic and terrified.

The plan was for Cam to get 8 hours of chemotherapy, for three days in a row, and then have two weeks off. There were no set number of cycles; essentially, they said this would continue until he or his body had had enough. After three cycles they would do more scans and tests to see if his cancer was responding to the chemo, as the type of sarcoma he had often didn't. After a night of not sleeping, I decided I wanted to get married right away before we learned anything else. I did not want to chance that the chemo wouldn't work, which I feared would result in all the joy of fulfilling our dream to be married being taken from our wedding day.

I woke poor Cam at 6am, just giddy with excitement and asked him if he would marry me in the next month. He smiled, kissed me and said, "Sure, hon, whatever you want." Then he went back to sleep. By this point Cam had already been calling me his wife, and introducing me as such for about 8 months so he figured the actual wedding was just a technicality; in his mind, we were already married.

I quickly set to work to find a Justice of the Peace and choose a date that worked. We settled on September 2, 2012 as our new wedding date. I had ten days to plan a wedding! Thankfully, I already owned "the dress", so that part was taken care of. At first we talked about not telling our families and just having it be a very intimate ceremony. Over the last month it had felt like there was no privacy, and everything about our lives was open for discussion. We wanted something that was just ours. But after a couple days we realized that while this was a very real desire, being a part of this wedding was likely very important for some of our family members, and that if our fears came true, this might be their only opportunity to witness us getting married.

We agreed on inviting our parents, siblings, my aunt, uncle and cousins, as well as Cam's best friend since they were seven years old, who was more like his brother. We told our bridal party that we had decided to get married in a small ceremony and would possibly still follow through on the June wedding, but wouldn't know until later. Thankfully, they were all more than understanding and supportive of our decision to move forward even if they couldn't be there as had been originally planned. We decided not to tell many people until right before the big day. On

August 31st I arranged a girl's night at a comedy club and dressed myself up in bachelorette gear from a dollar store. Eighteen amazing ladies came out and were surprised to learn I was getting married in two days! It was a great night. Cam and a huge group of his friends all went paintballing together that same night. The high of that night lifted some of the pain the previous month had settled on us.

Some of my friends have spoken of getting cold feet right before their wedding, or questioning whether they are making the right choice. For me there never was any questioning it, as Cam was always who I wanted. I only felt excitement that I was able to experience one of our dreams come true, that I was going to be married to my best friend, that cancer hadn't been able to cheat me from this dream, this wonderful experience. Cam told me afterwards that my dad had approached him while they were waiting for me to finish getting ready to come out and said that he looked completely calm, like he had done this before. Cam told me that he knew without a doubt that he wanted to marry me and hadn't felt nervous at all simply because there was nothing to be nervous about. I think for many people there are a lot of unknowns that suddenly come up when you decide to spend your life with someone.

For Cam and I were facing the scariest unknowns anyone could imagine and facing it together made it tolerable. Getting married, therefore, only alleviated fear for us. It was a beautiful, windy, outdoor ceremony; one during which we both, and others in attendance, had teary cheeks and plenty of laughs.

The Justice of the Peace said many wonderful things and we also asked him to do a reading from Beyond Words Daily Readings in ABC's of Faith;

> *"They say they will love, comfort, honor each other to the end of their days. They say they will cherish each other and be faithful to each other always. They say they will do these things not just when they feel like it, but even -- for better for worse, for richer or poorer, in sickness and in*

health -- when they don't feel like it at all. In other words, the vows they make could hardly be more extravagant. They take upon themselves each other's burdens. They bind their lives together... The question is, what do they get in return?

"They get each other in return... There will always be the other to talk to, to listen to... There is still someone to get through the night with, to wake into the new day beside. If they have children, they can give them, as well as each other, roots and wings. If they don't have children, they each become the other's child.

"They both still have their lives apart as well as a life together. They both still have their separate ways to find. But a marriage made in heaven is one where two people become more richly themselves together than chances are either of them could ever have managed to become alone."

-- Frederick Buechner

I also asked my mother to read the following script, which I had written, prior to us saying our vows:

Love is Forever

There are no guarantees in life. No two people, when they decide to spend their lives together, can possibly know how long 'forever' will be for them.

There are variables beyond our control. But love asks us to take a chance, to believe, to risk being hurt and to enjoy each day that we are given.

Cam and Leanne's union is no different; however, they have been made aware of how precious each moment they have together truly is.

They are aware that there aren't guarantees for any of us that tomorrow will come, and they have learned painfully to just be grateful for the love they have today.

Although the future is as uncertain as ever, today we come together to celebrate a love that has stood the test of many challenges, a love that refuses to back down in the face of fear, a love that surpasses this world and will last forever.

We celebrate their dedication to each other, to loving each other no matter what, and to their future together. May it be a long, happy and healthy one!

My vows:

I, Elizabeth Leanne, choose you, Cam, as my best friend, my love for life. I promise you my deepest love, my fullest devotion, my tenderest care; through the pressures of the present and the uncertainties of the future. I promise to be faithful to you. I pledge to respect your unique talents and abilities, to lend you strength and support for all of your dreams. I promise to try to remain positive and tell you my fears so we can deal with them together. I want to thank you for taking this journey with me over the last few years and for working with me to make our relationship healthy. Although this is a difficult time in our lives, and we have come to realize there are no guarantees, I promise to stand beside you no matter how bumpy or smooth the road ahead may be. I have no way of knowing what the future will hold, but I do know I love you and while love may not always be enough, it sure is a good place to start. I never expected to find someone I could not only love so very much, but trust to be my true self, in all its crazy, goofy glory, as well as unpleasantness. You taught me to love myself, you taught me that I am lovable and that I am worthy of your love. Today I marry my best friend, my inukshuk, my everything, and I know that I am the luckiest woman alive. I want you to know I have full trust in our relationship, full trust in you and full trust in our future. There is and really never was any looking back; I've always been yours, in heart and soul. I believe in you, Cam, and will be there for you always.

Cam's vows:

When we first started our journey together, it didn't take me very long to realize I was in love and wanted to spend the rest of my life with you. Some days are more challenging than others, but I always know somehow, some way we will figure things out. Now we are here getting married. Since we first met our lives have changed so much and we have grown as a couple, and as people. We have learned from each other, from both our good and bad qualities. We continue to build strength and our success in our relationship is shown with love. The key to our success is learning from our mistakes and always moving forward, more positive than the day before. I love your laughter and your ability to act goofy. You're my best friend and now you'll be my wife. I couldn't have asked for a better partner. I promise to continue being the person you love, with improvements to come along the way as we learn more everyday about each other. I'm happy you understand just how much I love you; that took some convincing!! I believe in you, and will support and motivate you in anything and everything you strive for. You're the person I look to for comfort. I know you'll always love me, and I will always love you. With love and effort we will create a beautiful life together.

We had decided that while we would invite our families to the ceremony, Cam and I would go to dinner on our own and have some much needed alone time. I will never regret this decision. After taking some pictures and eating cake, Cam and I jumped into my car and drove to Invermere, BC to spend two nights in a gorgeous condo there. The morning after our wedding, we woke up and found Cam's pillow covered in his hair. He ran his hand through it only to realize his hair was all falling out in clumps. Being a small town on Labor Day Monday, there was no hair salon open, so we went to Canadian Tire and bought a head shaving kit. In hindsight, I'm happy we were able to experience this on our own without anyone, even a hairdresser present, as it was very emotional for the both of us. There was no more pretending that he wasn't sick, that this wasn't now our life. We both cried as the first clumps of hair fell to the floor.

Chapter Six:
Summer Of Love

We had learned in the fall that the chemotherapy was working, the cancer was shrinking. Not that this meant Cam would get better, it was still palliative, but he would potentially have longer than originally expected. Initially, we had followed the doctor's orders to a tee. Cam avoided foods that contained antioxidants and vitamins, as there was the possibility they could interfere with chemo. After three months of treatments, in the fall of 2012, Cam was getting weaker and weaker. The chemotherapy was taking a toll on him. It was at this point we decided together that if the doctors had determined that he was going to die, and it was only a matter of time, then it didn't really matter if he followed their recommendations or not, so we might as well do some experimenting.

Cam began to follow the alternative treatment regimens I had researched in November 2012 (see Chapter Nine: The New Regime. Nonetheless, please note that I am not a doctor nor claim to know better than your doctor when it comes to medical advice. Please do your own research and consult with your doctor prior to making any changes). Within a month, we began to see improvements in his quality of life. Suddenly, the chemo no longer made him tired or nauseous. Cam was able to go to the gym five to six times a week and work out for two hours at a time, and he began to regain his strength and stamina. We began hiking regularly, even after a week of chemo treatments. He began to feel healthier than he ever had in his life. We never told the doctors what we were doing as we didn't want to hear what they might have had to say. The tests continued to show that the chemotherapy was working; the cancer continued to shrink.

May 21, 2013 felt like any other day when we woke up. It was a chemo week so we got up and drove to the Foothills Hospital to meet with Cam's oncologist and get his blood work done. The only thing that was different was that Cam had had a few scans done to see what was happening with the cancer and we would be getting those results. These were always hard days, both of us a bit more on edge; nervous, hopeful, scared, were all emotions that settled on us at the same time as we waited to hear how things were going. I still remember the confusion and then hesitant joy that began to fill me as the oncologist explained that the scans had shown no active cancer cells in Cam's body and that he no longer had to do chemotherapy.

While this had always been the goal, the fact that we had reached it, that we had done it was simply hard to compute. I must have asked the doctor two or three times if that meant we didn't have to come in the following day for chemo. I just felt it was all too good to be true. We left the hospital in a haze. However, about 20 feet outside the hospital doors, Cam stopped walking, looked at me and said, "We did it babe, we fucking did it!" He burst into tears as he pulled me into his arms. Anyone who saw us would have thought we had gotten horrible news because we cried uncontrollably and clung to each other. The absolute relief that washed over us was like nothing I have ever experienced before and likely never will again.

We had both tried so hard to make the best of our situation, and we had done a good job, we had found ways to be happy and have fun even if it required visits to the hospital and poison to be pumped into his veins. But fear is exhausting and we both were beyond exhausted. Every time Cam got chemo he said it would be the last time, that he couldn't keep doing this, that he didn't agree or believe in it and was only doing it out of fear and that he was just done. But then fear would win out and he would go to his next cycle. All of our worries about the future, exhaustion with the present, came flooding out of us as we stood there and cried for what we had gone through, and that we had made it out. Cam always gave me the credit, he had me on a pedestal and worshiped the ground I walked on, or at least that's how he made me feel. Through his tears he repeatedly thanked me for everything I had done, for making the juices, the shakes, the weird disgusting mushroom and root teas, all the tinctures, pills and vitamins. He sobbed as he thanked me for encouraging and walking with him to create a peaceful, holistic lifestyle where we practiced meditation daily, hiked every Sunday, did hot yoga throughout the week and went to a drumming circle on Friday nights. The chemo was never expected to get rid of the cancer, as that was never the goal. The goal of the medical world was simply to prolong his life. Yet here we were with results far better than the 'goal' and with no explanation other than all that Cam had done and changed in his life. While I know that many of the changes Cam made would not likely have happened had it not been for me, I also saw how much willpower and dedication it took on his part to follow through day in and day out. So I refused to take all the credit he tried to give me. As with everything, we were in it together. He got better because we worked as a team and he embraced a different lifestyle and outlook on life.

There is never a good time to get bad news, but man, was this ever the perfect time to get good news! On May 2nd we had found our almost dream home and put in an offer on May 3rd, which was accepted. I say it was our almost dream home, because we wanted an acreage, but couldn't afford it, and there were a few cosmetic things in the home that we wanted to upgrade. But we both knew we had found it when we had only seen the main floor and back yard. When we went into the basement and saw that it was finished but half of it was left open, Cam knew it was perfect as he wanted a space to work with his worm composting and indoor gardening. And when we went upstairs and into the master bedroom, I was ready to sign the paperwork right then as it was huge, with a large walk in closet, beautiful en suite with a big soaker tub and the view was simply stunning, as the house backed out onto a field, trees, and the river. No other houses in sight. Our acreage, without the work. We were due to get possession on May 27th and so hearing that the cancer was basically gone a week before moving into our new home allowed us to dream without holding back. Suddenly the future was full of promise, without the lingering fear that it might not come true.

Even though we were technically married, when it became apparent around Christmas that Cam would likely still be alive in the summer, we decided to move forward with our original wedding plans. This beautiful wedding was scheduled for June 29, 2013 just outside of Duncan, British Columbia on Vancouver Island at Maple Grove Guesthouse. We booked it over a year before Cam was diagnosed with cancer. Hearing that he was in remission could not have come at a better time. While our first wedding was special and oozed of commitment, love and dedication to each other, there was an underlying desperation and intense sadness. We were still excited to be marrying each other, still so happy and in love, but it wasn't the wedding we had been talking about for a year and a half. It wasn't with all our friends and family who we had originally wanted to be there, and it was happening because we had been told he likely would not be alive for our scheduled wedding date.

I hadn't even realized how paralyzed I felt when thinking about the future, how I had really embraced living in the moment as a way to be healthy, but also out of fear of the unknown. We got possession of our lovely farmhouse-inspired, Anne of Green Gables type home, and started the process of making it ours. Ripping up carpets and putting laminate hardwood flooring down, replacing all light fixtures and toilets, painting the whole house, Cam building a garden and buying bushes and tree after tree. And while we worked on the house together, I busily tried to make all the final arrangements for the wedding. Now it wasn't all happiness and roses. Life never is that way, and even with our wonderful news and the excitement of the future finally being something we both felt we could look at, we still dealt with everyday stress.

Moving is stressful. Renovations, no matter how minor, are stressful. Planning a wedding in a different province is stressful. So looking back (and hindsight is always 20-20) we did amazingly well, but in the moment there were days where both of us wondered what we had gotten ourselves into. There were times both of us felt the other wasn't pulling their weight, but it had much more to do with the difference in our priorities or what we wanted to see the other helping with, rather than the other actually not doing enough. I know that now. And I largely only know it now because I am trying to run our house on my own and realizing all the things Cam did without me having to nag at him, all the things that he did that I didn't even know existed or needed doing and thus never appreciated.

Similarly, he could not fathom the amount of time planning the wedding took, calling the vendors, answering questions of guests, making last minute arrangements, and on and on. So while that month was truly amazing, it also had its fair share of stress. Part of me can't help but smile at how quickly we can forget and start to take life for granted again. When he was obviously sick, when it was feared that he would die, and when we realized how very important it was to just be present with each other in everyday and be grateful for each moment, we really learned to question whether the fight was worth it.

Don't get me wrong, we bickered and nitpicked, but that was just us, and to others they would think it was often far more significant than it ever was. For the most part we would discuss, or as others perceived it, bicker over, something and then it would be sorted and we would move on. Cam was probably the most stubborn person I have ever met and I'm not far behind him, but our relationship always took precedence over being 'right'.

To add to this joy and stress (funny how at times in life they go hand in hand and the same thing can cause both emotions) was the fact that we had made it to the top of the fertility waiting list and were starting that process. While learning that Cam's cancer had vanished, and buying/renovating our first home together and getting ready for our second wedding which was weeks away, we were also having meetings with the fertility clinic about options, and I was undergoing numerous tests. Cam's sperm was safely frozen at the clinic and in a nonchalant way the doctor mentioned that Cam would have been the perfect donor as his sperm count was quite high and they were all active.

We laughed and cried about this later, as what good did that do us now? Chemotherapy had left him without a single sperm; he was infertile. We simply had the 13 frozen straws to utilize. His reassuring words and absolute love for me are still with me, as I remember him just holding me and saying, "It will be alright, babe, somehow it will work out. You're too amazing not to be a mother, don't worry, hon." This was after they told us that with only 13 straws there was a likelihood I wouldn't get pregnant as it can take numerous tries and often each attempt uses 3 straws. Our next option, which had a 60% success rate was in-vitro fertilization, cost $10,000 per attempt. I felt cheated. I could not understand how something that is natural and appears to happen to people so easily could possibly not be an option for us.

Cam refused to give up hope that we would have a child together, and he calmed me by reassuring me that we would do whatever it took to have that baby no matter how much it cost. So, it was decided in September or October we would do our first attempt and if it didn't take then, we would switch to in-vitro fertilization. His calm and absolute assurance that it would be fine and that by the following summer we would be parents or waiting for our child to be born, allowed me to just trust that he was right. We had been through enough and this dream wouldn't be stolen from us.

On June 20, 2013 southern Alberta suffered from heavy rainfall which resulted in devastating floods. Thousands of people lost their homes, vehicles, workplaces and many lost animals, and I believe there were even some deaths. It was a very difficult time and life as we all knew it changed drastically in a matter of hours. Our new home was only 5 houses down from the evacuation line and the beautiful field behind our home became a raging river. We were due to set out with all our wedding decorations towards Vancouver Island on June 24th , yet there were numerous road closures and sections of the highway had been washed away. I can't help but laugh at my own selfishness and self-centeredness, as people were stranded and had lost everything, but I was concerned about how I would get all my decorations to British Columbia (BC) if we had to fly. Fortunately we discovered that by going north up through Jasper we would be able to cross into BC on different, still drivable roads and make our way to Vancouver Island.

We decided that we would leave a day early and take an extra day to get there. Thankfully, once this was decided, we surrendered to it, and rather than being frustrated or annoyed by the extra driving, looked at it as a little pre-honeymoon. Cam had never been to Jasper and it had been years since I had been there. We rented a little cabin for one night which allowed dogs, as we were bringing Bentley with us; did two hikes; went out for a lovely dinner and wandered through the very touristy shops. While I would never wish the devastation of the floods on anyone, I am grateful that we were forced to slow our trip down and take an alternative, stunningly beautiful route. It set the tone for the rest of the trip to Victoria, which continued to be eating out at lovely restaurants, walking Bentley before setting out in the morning and arriving at our destination.

Our beautiful butterfly wedding. I don't know if words could ever describe how magical that weekend was. It felt like time stood still for a little while, as if it was that perfect bite of your favorite dessert that you can still taste long after having swallowed it. Early in the planning stages, I realized that it was custom to pick two colors and then coordinate the entire wedding around those colors. Much like many brides, I looked online and in magazines to get ideas, to try and find a color set that spoke to me. But it all felt so formal and not us. We could never be described by two colors, we were a full rainbow!

So, I decided that instead of picking two colors we would go with a butterfly theme and have them all! This fit perfectly. Butterflies often represent transformation and change; both of which our relationship had gone through plenty of. Little did I know when I made this decision what a significant role butterflies would come to play in our lives. Each of my four wonderful bridesmaids were given a list of colors and told they could choose their dress color except they all had to be different from each other. Purple, blue, red, and pink were the lucky chosen colors. I then took pictures of each dress and sent them to a lady I found on Etsy and created silk ties to match the colors of each dress for each groomsmen and on each tie she hand painted butterflies. They turned out simply stunning.

The venue, which was on Vancouver Island, was fantastic and beyond what either of us could have hoped for. We had seen 12 venues in 3 days when Cam flew to Victoria for Canada Day long weekend in 2011, and while I was okay with a couple of them, Cam stubbornly said he was not interested in anything we had seen. Then I found Maple Grove, online, the night before he was to return to Calgary, and called them. Sure enough, we were able to drive down and see the space before he flew out. Within minutes of pulling up Cam turned to me and said, "This is it, babe, it's perfect." And it was. I knew it as soon as we pulled through the gate and was thrilled we had finally agreed on a place. There are 21 acres of land with horses, goats, pigs, chickens, etc. You can stay in the stunningly beautiful guesthouse for three nights (the night before the wedding, wedding night, and one night after) and then everything else is outside. About a five minute walk through the big growth trees from the guesthouse is where the wedding reception was held. There was hardly any need for decorations as the natural surroundings were gorgeous, but the day before the wedding, a few wonderful ladies helped me turn the area into a butterfly haven, with butterflies hanging from the ceiling, strategically placed in all the bushes and trees as well as throughout the reception hall. Like I said, I cannot describe how simple and breathtaking it was all at once. My dad teased me that I had managed to buy every butterfly in North America, and yet forgot about getting a wedding cake. Yes, I forgot to order a wedding cake and realized this after the ceremony as we were doing pictures. Luckily, someone volunteered to drive to Dairy Queen and we had ice cream cake, which was the best wedding cake I've personally ever had!

They always say that your wedding day is the happiest day of your life and I really have to agree. This second wedding on June 29, 2013 was absolutely amazing! From the moment I woke up, I felt like there was nothing that could happen on that day that could possibly upset me; I was floating. As we were already married, we had asked one of our good friends to renew our vows and pulled from different ceremony readings to create the ceremony (see Appendix One for ceremony readings and vows).

I felt beyond loved, supported and was actually awestruck at how many people loved Cam and me. It was an amazing realization. At one point during the reception I stopped and just looked around at all the amazing people who had come so far to witness us renew our vows and commitment to each other. I felt so many emotions, and peace and gratitude were definitely up there on the list. I danced like I have never danced before. As neither of us drank, we didn't supply any alcohol, but some people brought their own. We had two big camp fires burning and the DJ played songs from the very long list I had provided him, which had us all jumping around and yelling out the words to old favorites and new hits. It was 29 degrees Celsius out and I was dripping in sweat, so a couple of the girls took their water bottles and drenched me and my wedding dress. I cannot remember a day where I laughed more fully or felt luckier.

The next day we invited everyone to come back and have a huge breakfast of scrambled eggs, hash browns and bacon. Then about 20 of us younger folk all drove further up island, rented inner tubes and floated down the Cowichan River, in 31 degree Celsius weather! Truly an epic way to end a wedding celebration weekend! Afterwards Cam told me, while crying, that it was the best weekend of his life and worth every penny (something that made me smile after all the arguments we had over the price of everything). It was the first time he and his four best friends, whom he had known since Elementary and Junior High, had ever gone away together, and all of them have since spoken about how much fun they had and that it was a great way to have a boy's weekend and hang out.

On the road trip back to Calgary we discussed the sad fact that due to the floods there were lots of people who had to give up their dogs as they had lost their homes. We decided to look into fostering dogs as Cam had been wanting to get a second dog for few months. I had been putting on the breaks as Bentley was largely my responsibility and I didn't want to add more to my plate. While Cam drove, I looked online and ended up sending in an application with the Animal Rescue Foundation in Calgary. Within a couple days we got a phone call, then I went through a phone interview which we passed and it was decided that a dog would be brought to our home on July 8th. And just like that Mickey entered our lives and snuck fully into our hearts. Cam, in particular, immediately fell in love with this dog from one of the reservations who had been semi-wild for the first three years of his life.

Mickey oozed gratitude and his most annoying habit was his desire to lick you repeatedly. Within two weeks we had decided to take in other dogs and had two 6 week old puppies that had been found on a reservation without their mom. For the next few months we had anywhere from four to six dogs and puppies in our home, as we found adoptive homes for them. It wasn't easy to let the puppies go, but there was always another little fur ball needing love to take their place. However, with Mickey, his personality was developed, and he was a fantastic dog. So when we got an application for his adoption and I told Cam and saw his eyes well with tears, I knew we were going to be adopting him. After Cam had passed, I was reading a journal he wrote in and on July 27, 2013 he wrote "I love my life and my growing family! Today was a great day, we get to keep Mickey. I love the pups so much."

While two dogs is a lot of work and the boys do not always see eye to eye, I have never regretted this decision as those two dogs bring me so much joy and brought Cam so much love and laughter while he was here. They were his constant companions when I wasn't around and they have saved my life in many ways by demanding I get out of bed, get exercise every single day and by showering me in love.

Life was perfect. I know it is common to look back and glorify how wonderful things were when in reality they weren't as good as we remember them. But we knew how perfect it was, and we didn't take one second for granted. We loved, and we loved deeply. Cam started working as an electrician again, and while we were both working full time, we managed to fill our spare time with hikes in the mountains and playing with the dogs and numerous puppies that graced our home.

In August we decided to go to Waterton with our dogs and spend a few days doing hikes. In five days we hiked 59km with approximately 3,275 meters elevation gain and we felt fantastic. Both of us were in the best shape of our lives and felt healthier than could ever be explained. On one of the hikes Cam turned to me and said, "Babe, let me finish before getting upset, but I was wondering what you thought about waiting till December to start trying to get pregnant. I am having so much fun with it just being us and the dogs, we have the rest of our lives to be parents. Can we just enjoy the time where it's just us and have fun for a bit?"

And so, it was decided that we would put off our first attempt at getting pregnant as there no longer was any rush, at least that we knew of. Laying in our tent with our two pups snuggled up on our feet, we talked about our dreams for the future, and we spoke life to all the things we hadn't dared talk about while he was sick, while our future seemed so uncertain. And we had hope again, pure and utter joy and hope. It was our summer of love, our summer of dreams coming true, our summer of reprieve. I'll forever be grateful we were given that break, given the chance to hope and laugh in the carefree way only those who are not plagued with fear can.

Chapter Seven:
Living In An Hourglass

Life was perfect, as close to perfect as anyone can ever really hope for. We had a gorgeous home that we couldn't wait to start growing into. Both of us were working at jobs we had studied to become and enjoyed. We had two amazing dogs and a stream of adorable wiggly foster puppies to keep us busy and make us laugh. Cam was cancer free, we had beat it, the impossible had seemingly occurred. He had beat stage four sarcoma. We had met with the fertility doctors, I had done all the tests needed and we had chosen the month for our first attempt to become pregnant. Cam and I were in better shape than either of us ever had been in our lives. We spent long hours climbing various mountains near our home, in Canmore, Banff and Watertown every weekend. We appreciated every day and felt like life had given us another chance and we were going to enjoy every second of it.

On September 8, 2013 Cam suffered the first headache. He had suffered with migraines on and off for as long as we had been together, so I didn't think anything of it. Cam was adamant that this was not like any migraine he had ever had, that it was far more painful, that he hadn't had light flashes in his eyes to warn him it was coming; rather, it suddenly felt like his brain was growing inside his skull and was threatening to burst out. He left work early the next day and struggled through the pain to drive home. He called in sick the day after that and by the 13th, Cam called and quit for he realized that something was terribly wrong.

By this point the headaches would come on with such intensity he would scream with pain, tears streaming down his face, holding his head, throw up, and shake violently while sweating so much the sheets on our bed would be soaked. I prayed that first week it was a change in the weather, that there was some external explanation. He went to the doctor the first week on his own and reported back to me that he was to watch the headaches and that he had been told it sounded like the cause was stress. I questioned exactly what Cam had told the doctor as that sounded ridiculous, but Cam was not himself and angered very quickly. I know that when I am in pain my patience is very limited and I often lash out at the ones I love, but there was an element of snarky meanness to Cam that I had never known. It was to the point that by a week after the headaches started I was scared to oppose him and felt like I was walking on egg shells because the slightest thing could set him off. I did not know the man I was sharing a bed with anymore, and I didn't understand what had changed or why things had changed. The pain became so unbearable that one night lying in bed with the lights off Cam began to speak in a way that triggered all my senses.

As a family counsellor in addictions and mental health I work with many individuals who struggle with thoughts of suicide and am trained in suicide risk assessments. So listening to the man who I loved more than anyone else in the world, I became acutely aware of the warning signs. I finally asked him if he was planning on killing himself and he broke down crying that he couldn't live in this pain anymore. He needed it to stop.

He laid in my arms and sobbed, while apologizing but explaining that it hurt too much and not being able to escape the pain was unbearable and made him feel like he was going crazy. He told me his plan, all of which was detailed and thought out. Now for anyone who knew Cam, the idea that he struggled with thoughts of suicide would seem insane, for he loved life and lived it to the fullest. For me, it was the largest slap across my face that something was horribly wrong, confirmation that my greatest fear had to be right, the cancer had to be back and it had to have gone to his brain. I knew there was no way he would ever normally want to die, but being in such constant, unrelenting pain had driven him to his breaking point and all he could think about was escaping it, even if that meant giving up what he had just fought so hard to achieve. Cam went to the doctor three times and I brought him to emergency twice in the first three weeks of his headaches, but every time he was simply given pain meds and told to take up anti-stress activities, that the past year of his life struggling with cancer had likely caught up with him and was resulting in headaches. I feared Cam wasn't being honest with how severe things were and took it upon myself to call his doctor and set up a private conversation that Cam was not to know about as I feared he would be angry at me for going behind his back. I outlined the progression of symptoms, explained the severity of them and that Cam was now thinking about ending his life due to the level of pain he was experiencing. I was also very direct that I knew the cancer was back, and from the mood changes and intense headaches, believed it had gone to his brain. The next week he was scheduled to have an MRI of his body and the following week a CAT Scan of his brain. Even though I knew in my heart it was back, nothing could prepare me for the news I was about to hear.

On September 27, 2013 I went to work and Cam went to get his MRI. It was a Friday. We didn't expect to hear the results until our next appointment with his oncologist on October 7th. When my phone rang during my supper break while I ate in the staff room and saw it was Cam, I didn't think anything of it. But when I heard his voice, heard him say that the cancer was back and had spread throughout his body, heard the words "I lit up like a Christmas tree", I felt defeated.

It is one thing to hear that you have cancer. Absolute terror ranks through your body and you feel paralyzed. Suddenly all your givens and dreams become questionable. You have no idea what you're up against and the unknown is horrible. But when you have gone through it, when you believe to have overcome it and then hear it is back, you know what you're dealing with. You know just how exhausting, time consuming, draining and unimaginably horrific it is. And you don't know if you have the energy or ability to do it all again. Sometimes knowing the enemy is worse than simply fearing the unknown.

While feeling all this, I reassured Cam in a steady voice that at least we knew what to do this time to get rid of it and would just have to get serious again with his regime which we had let go to a certain extent so he could enjoy various forbidden foods again. I spoke with Cam for a few minutes and then let him go telling him how much I loved him and that we would get through this just like we did the last time. I hope I sounded more convincing than I felt. I immediately called my mom and as soon as I heard her voice, I broke into sobs through which I managed to tell her the cancer was back. My sobs brought concerned co-workers to the staff room. I'm very lucky to work with a bunch of counsellors as I did not need to worry about keeping my composure or what any of them might have thought.

I was supposed to run a therapy group at 6pm for teenagers and was trying to figure out how I would hold it together for an hour when they simply told me that I needed to leave work and go be with Cam and that they would take care of the group. Looking back, it's odd that I wouldn't have thought of that myself, but I had never called in sick to work a day in my life, nor left work early, so the thought that I even could leave really hadn't crossed my mind. I took the next four days off and Cam and I spent them crying, holding each other, letting all our fears spill out of our mouths and then devising a plan to tackle what we knew lay ahead. We had a rule that we were allowed two days to fall apart and live in fear, then we had to snap out of it, get positive and appreciate that we had still had today and that is all any of us are ever really promised.

Just when we were feeling like it was doable, had the vitamins and needed ingredients to start him back on his regime, it came time for his CT scan of his brain. Cam was still throwing up daily and in unimaginable pain to the point where he had to be driven to the hospital to have the test done as he was too sick to drive himself as had been the original plan. It was October 3, 2013. I remember work was supposed to have a potluck and a co-worker and I were trying to find the room in the hospital unsuccessfully, so we returned to my office to check the email. I checked my phone while there and saw three missed calls from Cam in the last few minutes. Thinking that odd and knowing how sick he had been earlier, I called him back. I still feel the chills throughout my body that his words gave me; ".The doctor called and it's in my brain. I have 30 tumors in my brain".

I had been prepared for it to be in his brain. I knew that my first prediction had been right, that it was back and had even intensified my belief that it was now in his brain. But 30 tumors? That I simply could not understand. I asked for clarification that I heard right, told him I had expected one or two, not 30, and sat in shock. We knew how to handle cancer, but I did not know how to handle brain cancer and I certainly didn't know how to handle a cancer that had gone from remission in late May to suddenly taking over the entire body and brain by late September. It is no wonder his pain was so unbearable with all those tumors growing and taking up room; his brain literally was pressing against his skull. My co-worker came back into my office to see if I had got the correct room number and I was sitting in the dark looking down at the desk, tears quietly flowing down my face. I told her what I had just learned and somehow that made it real, somehow uttering the words out loud meant it really was happening. I know I cried a lot. I know my supervisor came in and my co-worker had to explain what was happening because I couldn't speak, I was crying so hard. That with each passing moment I realized the sand in our hourglass was flowing faster and faster and there might be nothing I could do to slow it down. I left work and somehow managed the drive. I think by then I had mastered driving with tears streaming down my face.

Cam met me outside on the front porch and flung himself into my arms, both of us soaking each other's shirts with our tears. I still remember how it felt like I was being physically stabbed every time I told someone about the tumors in his brain and the look that would come over their face, the absolute shock, pity and sadness; as if he was already dead or as good as dead. I wanted to scream at people that it didn't have to be a death sentence, to not give up on him, yet every cell in my body was terrified they were right.

Journal entry from October 4, 2013, the day after we learned it went to his brain.

Change

Life is always changing, there is no constant. All I have ever known is change and yet it is the thing I fear the most. It has blessed me, I have clung to it and I promise it to others. Promise if they, if I, can only hold on a bit longer it will pass, things will change. But what I don't say, what I dare not say out loud is that change is not always good, it does not always mean peace or happiness. And it is most definitely not always easy. So yes, I sit here as my world spins around me, as I grab at things to hold onto, moments to remember, sights, sounds, tastes and feelings which I will treasure once change occurs and they are gone. I am grateful for change, as without it I wouldn't be me. I wouldn't be where I am now, wouldn't have let go and moved on, and made choices I needed to in order to change. But I fear it and wish I could push pause or rewind just for a little while, just to really get to enjoy the now because it slips and changes faster then I want it to, faster than I fear I can handle. My future has the potential to be so bright, so many options ahead of me, but how do I look forward to a future that promises so many changes, changes I do not want to face?

After our allotted fall apart days, Cam and I began to plan how we would move forward. The doctors suggested radiation on his brain as well as a couple different medications to decrease the swelling in his brain. Thankfully, these medications were almost immediately effective and the headaches decreased substantially. We were able to do a few more short hikes and enjoy the beautiful Indian Summer Calgary was enjoying. The last week of October we went with my aunt and uncle to one of our favorite hiking spots with our dogs and our last foster puppy who was going to her adoptive home later that day. Little did we know that it would also be the last hike Cam would ever have the strength to do, but even if we had known, I couldn't have asked it to have been any more perfect.

We had lunch at our normal resting spot, a large rock surrounded on three sides by alder trees and facing the full range of the Rocky Mountains. As was common, we called for a moment of silence and even the air seemed to stand still, time stopped and the magic of the moment, the peace I felt amidst all the chaos in my life resulted in silent tears escaping my eyelids. A couple months later, Cam asked to have his ashes scattered at this rest stop, and on what would have been our one year anniversary of our beautiful butterfly wedding. A group of us granted this wish.

Cam was adamant that he did not want to know what his prognosis was, that no one was going to tell him when he would die. I, on the other hand, wanted to know so that I could prepare myself. Yet nothing will ever prepare you to hear that your husband will likely see Christmas a mere 10 weeks away, but anything after that is not guaranteed and that he definitely would not have more than six months.

I learned that heart wrenching news on October 9th. I went on disability leave from work the following day and did not return until six weeks after he had passed away, which in hindsight was still too soon for me. Deciding to stay home with Cam rather than trying to work was the best decision I could have made, one I'm grateful for every day. We tried to create a lifetime of memories in a short time. On the days his energy was good, we would take advantage of it by going out and doing things, and on the days he was weaker we would snuggle up and watch Netflix with our dogs. I made it my mission to make him laugh every day, to do everything in my power to ease any pain he had, to find foods that didn't cause as much discomfort and to just soak up every minute

I could because I knew they were running out. Every day was the opportunity for new memories to be created, I didn't have the luxury of looking forward to the future or making plans and, in a way, this forced me to be creative in the moment, to appreciate every hug and smile.

We went to Mexico from November 3rd to the 10th with his dad and stepmom. Neither of us had ever been to Mexico and we were very excited. The first three days there were amazing. We released squiggly baby turtles into the ocean and squealed with delight and concern as they struggled across the sand. We all went shopping and ate at amazing restaurants both on and off the resort. Some of my favorite memories there were when we swam in the ocean, played in the waves, splashed each other and bounced around.

Yet all of that changed on November 6th. He woke up in the night throwing up and continued to throw up like clockwork almost every two hours. Being in Mexico, there was the possibility that he had eaten something that did not agree with him or his compromised immune system had allowed him to catch something that didn't affect the rest of us. At this point he hadn't thrown up from headaches since he had started dexamethasone which decreased the swelling in his brain. When the throwing up continued into the second day, we all began to become concerned. I would make him drink electrolytes and any food he could handle after throwing up and give him Tylenol and Gravol in quantities that far exceeded the recommended doses.

This resulted in him appearing to come in and out of consciousness and at times was simply impossible to wake up. At the time we did not know if it was the amount of medication that was causing him to be so sleepy or if he was beginning the process of dying. His legs overnight had become so weak that he was unable to walk and needed a wheelchair to get from the resort onto the plane home and then to the car. We went from playing in the waves one day to not knowing if he would make it home alive while watching his eyes roll into the back of his head when I would try to talk to him the day after.

For anyone who has been intimately involved in the care and life of someone transitioning from this world, you know of all the losses. They do not simply die in one day. No, there are multiple small deaths, losses along the way that hurt more than anyone not closely involved may ever understand. I remember sitting on the balcony of our hotel room watching the third wedding that day going on below. Tears streamed down my face as I looked at all the beautiful colors and smiling faces. My heart broke as I looked through the screen door at Cam asleep in bed, unmoving with the garbage can propped beside him and pill cases lining the bedside table. I remember realizing in that moment that nothing would ever be the same; that I had lost my husband, that what I thought of as husband and wife pair was no longer, that we had entered a new realm, that I was now his caregiver.

I expect my husband to help around the house, I expect it to be an equal marriage, to give as much as you receive, and yet that was no longer possible. I no longer could expect anything from Cam, and yet would give everything I could because I loved him more than I ever knew it was possible to love another human. But I lost my husband, my equal, my partner on that trip and I became the decision maker, I realized I needed to step up and be his voice when he wasn't able to.

Being someone's advocate isn't an easy job. Being an advocate when that person sometimes forgets that they agree with you or have asked you to be their voice of reason places you in a very difficult spot. There were many times I felt that I had to be the 'bitch' because Cam would beg me to ensure he didn't eat the foods that caused him pain, but then in moments of weakness he would want to follow the longing of his taste buds. And when I tried to stop him, he would become extremely angry.

I could not win these fights, for if I let him eat the food as soon as the pain started, which on average no one else would see, he would then be angry at me for 'allowing' him to eat it. And if I managed to not let him eat the food, he would be angry for the next few hours at me for trying to 'control' him and restricting his ability to enjoy life. Food was literally the only thing we fought over those last few months and was the focus of so much struggle. Part of me desperately wanted to allow Cam to eat anything and everything he wanted because if he didn't have long to live, then he should be able to enjoy it fully. But the reality that I lived in daily was that all those foods he loved so much only brought momentary joy, and then I was left hearing him in pain. No one else had to see this reality, no one else had to live it and thus no one understood it, or why I was so obsessed with everything that went into his mouth. I often felt undermined by others who simply did not understand, as their only concern was making Cam happy in the moment and giving him whatever he wanted.

This was a luxury I was not allowed, and I felt wildly jealous that they could be the 'good' guys who brought him things he loved and then I had to decide whether to deal with the pain later and let him eat it, or be his advocate and step in and explain that he could not have it. The latter often resulted in Cam, and whoever the person was, being angry with me. So yes, I was his advocate, and it is a job I would never wish on anyone, one I would do again in a second because I know he needed it, but God, all I wanted was to be his wife, to be equal. But that option was gone and I refused to live in denial, so I accepted that I would make many people angry at me for the decisions I would make about Cam's care; that in the end it didn't matter as long as I knew in my heart I made every decision with my best friend's interests as the sole purpose. I could deal with the whole world hating me, even with Cam being angry at me, as long as I knew I had done all I could to take care of him. No, being an advocate is not an easy job, and it calls for hard decisions to be made numerous times a day.

After Mexico, Cam was struggling to go to the washroom on his own, especially if he ate anything that wasn't on his allowed foods list. This obviously caused incredible amounts of pain and even stool softeners and laxatives didn't seem to help much. We then discovered coffee enemas and they were a God send! I have no idea if Cam's response to the coffee enemas was typical and thus cannot guarantee others would have a similar experience. After breakfast and dinner, I would prepare and give Cam a coffee enema to stimulate bowel movements and help manage the pain (see Appendix Two). I often marvel at how lucky we were that we were so comfortable with each other, and that there was never any questioning whether I would be the one to lubricate the hose before inserting it into his rectum and draining the liter of warm coffee into his colon and intestines. There were days when he couldn't walk; where he wasn't able to bear his own weight to get out of bed, I would give him an enema, and for the next five or six hours he could walk short distances around the house or to the car. Anything more than 10-20 minutes of walking we would take the wheelchair, which increased both of our understanding of just how unfriendly our world is to those with physical disabilities. Not only did the enemas somehow decrease the pain he was feeling to the point where he could start to walk again, but they also made it possible for him to come off of all the different pain medications that the doctors had prescribed him.

Any time he would start to have a headache or pain in any part of his body, we would do an extra enema and it simply disappeared. They were our saving grace, the thing that I truly believe allowed him to be able to stay home and in my care, rather than in hospice until he passed away.

Cam had to spend a week in hospital getting re-stabilized after our trip to Mexico. Embracing life and the time we had, we decided to not let fear get in our way and hopped on another plane after he was discharged and went to Victoria to visit my family, who were living there at that time. We had an incredible week, seeing my friends from when I had lived there, and hanging out with my family. Everyone got the opportunity and privilege of knowing the new version of Cam, where he wasn't worried about appearing 'cool' and would cry or just be honest about how he felt. As my then-eight year old sister said after he passed away, "Every time I saw Cam, I liked him more and more. It's sad he had to die."

Cam hadn't known how to interact with my very young siblings when he first met them, but as he grew comfortable with them over the years and realized he didn't have time to worry whether he looked silly, he allowed himself to just have fun, to be a kid again. I remember each of my siblings hugging Cam goodbye at the end of the trip and how he cried about it afterwards saying that they didn't even hesitate, that he felt like he was actually a part of the family and not just the guy that I brought with me.

We also had a lot of time to relax in Victoria. The hotel we stayed at overlooked the ocean and was quite simply the most gorgeous place either of us had stayed. We scheduled three different spa days and had massages, facials, as well as foot and leg massages. Cam began to regain some of his strength and we spent time in the infinity pool that over looked the ocean, as well as the hot tubs that also were outside by the ocean every day. It was in one of these hot tubs that we last made out. We had not been intimate in a long time as the cancer and the radiation used to shrink the tumors had destroyed his libido. I still remember it perfectly, remember laying in his arms laughing and talking, the entire place to ourselves. When life is stressful you learn to seek moments of reprieve and joy. This was one of those times. I splashed around in the hot tub until he pulled me to him and we kissed for a few minutes. I still can remember how thirsty I felt for him, how much longing was behind those kisses, longing that never would be met. But for those minutes it felt like we were a 'normal' young married couple on vacation and unable to keep our hands off each other.

On December 11, 2013 we celebrated our 5th year of being together as a couple. It was hard to imagine all we had been through as a couple in 5 years. We stayed in Canmore, Alberta for two nights in order to celebrate. Two days in a row we went to the spa for various luxurious treatments, as I had made the decision that I, who had always been worried about money, would not concern myself with how I would get by after Cam was gone; all that mattered was doing things together that Cam was able to do and we found fun or relaxing. So yes, we went to the spa a lot those last couple months and I wouldn't have had it any other way.

On our anniversary we went on a one-horse open sleigh ride in the bitter cold but snuggled together under about twenty blankets and had an absolute blast. Every meal was somehow better than the last and all were somehow within the foods that were allowed! It truly was the best anniversary we could have asked for. Some Facebook messages we each posted that day:

Cam: "In Canmore having my anniversary. I have been with the most amazing woman for five years and married for just a little bit less lol. We made it past a year thankfully! She is my world and my love! To the end of time, and no matter what happens in this journey, the strength we share is beyond comprehension. I love you, Elizabeth Leanne, you're my rock! You keep me grounded and happy."... and then "Leanne, I love you more than anything, this isn't a Facebook goodbye, just a global Facebook message to let everyone know how much you mean to me and how dedicated you are to me. YOU'RE my WORLD, my Everything, and I love love love you so very deeply words are hardly enough to express how phenomenal a human being you are."

Me: "I cannot believe that 5 years ago today I was spontaneously and very anxiously getting together with my best friend who I hadn't seen in 8 years! My biggest worry was whether I should shave my legs or if that would be too presumptuous. Lol. Who knew that not only would meeting up rekindle our amazing friendship but would lead to a love so deep and strong that it has been able to stand the test of things I could not have even understood or imagined at that time. Love you so much, Cam! p.s- I didn't shave and apparently that didn't matter. (wink emoticon) Love is love regardless of the amount of hair on our heads, legs or bodies, at least for this crazy couple!"

Anyone who has either been sick themselves or been a caretaker for someone who is, you know how slowly, and at times quickly, your social life changes. How other people's lives continue and how they simply do not know where they fit, do not want to impose, do not want to see illness as it reminds them that their happy simple life could disappear at any moment, reminds them nothing is safe and there is absolutely nothing they can do about it. Or, at least, this is what I assume went on in many people's minds as they slowly withdrew.

There were moments where Cam missed his old social life, missed having the freedom to come and go as he pleased, but I think it was me who was more upset than he. Somehow, Cam understood and accepted that not everyone can stand in the fire with another and not shrink back. But I never saw an option. This was my fire just as much as it was his even if in the end somehow I survived it. So, I tried to have parties to celebrate the holidays, to get our friends together, to allow an opportunity for people to see Cam and not feel that they had to figure out what to say all on their own. In October we had two parties where people came over and carved pumpkins. And on December 15th we had a gingerbread house party. Our friends came over with food and everyone brought a gingerbread house making kit. Cam had been acting weird, but I figured it was due to the amount of people over and that he was overwhelmed, as had started happening in social situations. I gave him his kit and told him to open it; however, he just looked around the room with a huge smile on his face until he got up and walked into a different room with some of his friends.

It wasn't till later that I would realize that his weird behavior was a warning sign of his brain starting to shut down, of what was coming. I remember standing in the kitchen with beaters making more icing sugar, remember hearing my name screamed over and over by various voices and thinking that they were being very demanding for icing sugar. I remember coming around the corner to our living room and seeing my darling Cam on the floor convulsing, remember knowing without a doubt he was having a seizure, even though I've never seen one. I will forever be grateful for all the people who stepped up and did what I told them, as well as taking matters into their own hands that day. 911 was called, people went out and moved vehicles so that the ambulance would have somewhere to park, furniture was moved, my dogs put outside and taken care of once we left, people helped me roll Cam onto his side and brought paper towel when he threw up. To those who stayed and cleaned my house, to the person who put their hand on my back letting me know I wasn't alone as I sat beside my unconscious convulsing husband, I will forever be grateful.

We had bought the most amazing ugly Christmas sweaters and were both wearing them. I knew the ambulance crew would simply cut it off, so once the seizure had stopped, I carefully undid the buttons. People gently teased me that in the midst of chaos I was worried about saving the sweater, but for me I knew all that could be done had been done and somehow focusing on each button gave me something to do, kept me from falling apart when I knew I had to be strong. He had a total of four major seizures that afternoon before the ambulance crew (who did cut off his t-shirt but not the sweater) gave him an injection to stop them. I rode with the ambulance to Calgary while people stayed to pick up the pieces at our home and to pack things I figured I might need; that they would later bring to me. There is no explaining the joy that filled my heart when his eyes started to open as they pulled into the Foothills hospital. And similarly, there is no way to ever explain the excruciating pain I felt when I realized he had lost parts of his long-term memory as well as very short term memory.

He was confused about why he was in hospital, what had happened. When it was explained to him that he had just had four seizures, he was filled with fear and confusion. When the nurse explained that this wasn't that uncommon with brain cancer, and I realized he did not remember his diagnosis, I had the simple thought that nothing was more unfair than having to re-tell him this horrible news. I had to explain to this man who had been through so much already that he had cancer, it had spread to his brain, how he had had seizures but doctors were treating him, and that he was going to be okay. I had to do this every few minutes, for the first few hours he was awake. And every time, I wanted to throw up. Every time, I saw the loss of hope, the terror, the devastation take over him. Somehow, I managed to put my own emotions aside and tried to console him as he learned this devastating news for the 'first' time over and over again. I held him as he cried and talked about how scared he was, of how much he didn't want to die, begged me to tell him that he wouldn't die.

We spent another week in hospital, but were very happy when he was allowed to leave and we could have Christmas at home as we had planned. Christmas was amazing! My mom and our extended family, along with Cam's parents and siblings, all came over to our house for our first Christmas in our home. I felt so mature, like such a grown-up with everyone sitting around my dining room table laughing. I will forever treasure those memories.

However, not all was easy during that time. The seizures had put a lot of pressure on Cam's brain, had changed how he controlled his emotions. Once again I saw drastic personality changes begin to take place, just as I had in September before he was diagnosed. Cam became frustrated very easily, he angered with little warning and was next to impossible to console or reason with. During these episodes, I had to constantly remind myself that it wasn't Cam, this wasn't the man I had fallen in love with. Thankfully, they were only episodes and would come on with little to no warning and end just as suddenly. Cam would cry and apologize afterwards for everything he said. He explained that it was like he could watch himself saying things to me and yet couldn't stop himself; as if he was trapped inside his angry, changing body. Slowly, but with effort, he learned to start to identify when the change was coming and warn me to get away from him. And he would go and do his own thing until the change had passed. I smile and marvel at the strength of this man's love for me and his desire to protect me, even from himself.

Together, we learned how to maneuver around his changing mind and body. We always said that we would work as long as we were willing to work at it. Our absolute love and devotion to each other gave us strength to get through the unimaginable, and fall in love with each other all over again each day as the sand in our hour glass quickly emptied.

Chapter Eight:
Hope For A Different Tomorrow

I have never been much of an event planner, never liked to have to organize things, and especially hated asking people for money. Yet love and the need to feel like you can actually do something when your world begins to spin out of control changed all that for me. It all started shortly after Cam began to lose his hair from the chemotherapy treatments. Neither of us expected it to affect us so much, but it was a constant reminder that he was sick. I decided that I would shave my head, I would stand with him, and thus, Naked in Solidarity was born.

I wanted my hair to be donated to an organization that could use it to make wigs and consequently realized I would have to allow it to grow a bit longer, which also would grant me time to plan the event. A few days after coming up with the idea someone mentioned that I could probably raise a lot of money if I wanted to. Through the hours and hours I spent researching sarcoma up to this point it had become increasingly clear that, due to it being a rare form of cancer, very little funds were put into researching it and consequently very little was understood about how people get it, how to prevent it, or how to treat it. And all of this resulted in very few people surviving. I was determined that if I could not make a difference in Cam's recovery, I would do everything in my power to ensure other families in the future had a different story to tell when they got this diagnosis.

I contacted the Alberta Cancer Foundation and discussed my desire to raise money, and I wanted all of the money raised specifically to go towards sarcoma research. A charity with exactly this purpose already existed and thus I agreed that all monies raised from Naked in Solidarity would go towards this Fund. With so little known about this cancer, it was more important to me at that time that we stand together, than to separately try to raise money. Planning the event was more work than I could have expected, but it all paid off in the end. On September 22, 2013 over 70 people came to my father in-law and his partner's acreage, to support Cam and I. Lunch and drinks were served, as well as a raffle draw for 15 different baskets that had been put together with donated goods. Prior to shaving my head, I managed through my tears to thank everyone for coming.

"I want to thank you all again for coming out today and supporting us. These past 14 months have been the most difficult and rewarding of my life. We all know that there is no such thing as forever and that, in theory, we should just live for today. However, I did not and I don't think could have fully appreciated how important it is to enjoy every day, at least a little, until I was faced with the possibility of losing the person who I had chosen to spend all my days with. Being given a diagnosis of cancer for anyone is terrifying. Being told that it is sarcoma, a very rare soft tissue cancer that only 50% of people survive a year, puts an entire new spin on the importance of life. Hearing all this at 27 years of age, when you are really just starting your life is simply confusing. July 22nd, 2012, the night we first learned it was cancer and that it had metastasized throughout Cam's body, was the most terrifying day and night of my life. Learning the type and severity of his cancer in early August left me feeling helpless and paralyzed. I am grateful every day that Cam and I did not remain paralyzed and refused to submit to his diagnosis. Every time we met with doctors, and left feeling discouraged and hopeless, we allowed ourselves two days to cry uncontrollably and discuss his 'impending' death.

Then it was time to snap out of it and get back to living. I strongly believe this healthy balance of accepting the possibility of death, while refusing to believe it had to be a reality, gave us strength to continue. There have been some very dark days along the way, and I will remain forever grateful to those of you who were there for me whether it was to just hold me while I cried about all the 'what ifs' and my fears; or helped distract me from my life by continuing to engage me in yours. And for those of you who helped out by walking Bentley, cooking us meals, sending food, constantly including us in prayers and financially assisting us, we could not have made it through without you. It would have been much harder to stay as positive as we have, had it not been for all the little and big things you did. Coming up with the idea to shave my head, and then deciding to create Naked in Solidarity as an event, was actually pretty simple. I don't think either Cam or myself expected to be quite as affected by his hair loss as we were. But when, on September 3rd, the day after our little wedding ceremony, his hair began to fall out it, was the first concrete realization of the reality we were living in. He didn't look sick and so we could pretend, but there is no pretending when your hair starts to fall out. There is no pretending when you're bald and it wasn't your choice. You're reminded of that every time you look in a mirror. Cam did a very good job of acting like it didn't upset him, and so many of you may not have realized how difficult it really was.

But I did. I knew it wasn't his choice to be bald. I knew how hard it was for him to never be able to escape the reality that he had cancer when looking in the mirror. I will hopefully never fully understand what that feels like as I do have a choice today. But as with so many things, I choose to stand fully beside Cam and those who also didn't have a choice. I have been told I'm brave so many times as

I have raised money over the last year; however, for me it's not bravery that allows me to stand here. It is love and dedication to my best friend, it's passion to actually be able to do something and make some difference, as I have felt beyond powerless over the last year. When I realized how hard losing his hair was for him, there was no other option in my eyes other than to join Cam, to stand naked together. Now, that doesn't mean I'm not scared to say goodbye to my hair, as it is a bit of an identity; however, I'm far more passionate about walking beside this man I love so much than I am afraid of how I will look or the stares I might get. Thank you all for coming to support me, for coming to support Cam and for helping us raise money so that in the future families who are given the dreadful diagnosis of sarcoma, it isn't as paralyzing. My hope to stand in solidarity is coming true, because all of you have chosen to care, have chosen to support a different story for the next person. Thank you. Alright let's do this thing!"

And with that I sat on a lawn chair and a hairdresser shaved my head! I was gladly surprised that I have a very lovely bald head! Cam, who had begun to grow his hair again, as he was still technically in remission at that time, also shaved off his hair. Sadly, we found out five days later that the cancer was back and he had to start treatments again, so his hair never got the chance to grow again. Along with us, my uncle and cousin also shaved their heads, which meant so much to Cam and me. And to our surprise, two other people who had heard of what I was planning to do stepped forward, the guy fully shaving his head and the girl cut 14 inches off her hair for a wig. It was a beautiful day and very moving. And to our absolute excitement we raised $9,421.00!

They say it only takes one person to change the world and I strongly believe that. We never can know or understand the impact our actions may have on others. My little sisters who were 11 and almost 8 at the time were inspired by my decision to shave my head and decided they too wanted to make a difference. In November 2013, when Cam and I went to Victoria to visit my family and friends, we spoke to my sisters' schools about the kind of cancer Cam had and why I had chosen to shave my head.

Both of my sisters hoped that their classmates would become interested and want to fundraise for sarcoma research by doing their own cut-a-thon. My 11 year old sister's school took up the challenge and began organizing Glenlyon Norfolk School Cut-a-thon, where students and teachers could shave their heads or cut off a minimum of 12 inches of hair to be donated for wigs. Two nights before Cam passed away, I spoke with my sister on the phone and she excitedly told me that they had raised $2,000 already, and that the different classrooms were having a friendly competition for which class could raise the most money. Cam shouted 'whoot whoot' in encouragement, as it meant so much to him that his little sisters-in-law were putting so much effect into raising awareness and money.

Sadly, Cam passed away two weeks before the cut-a-thon was scheduled, but I was able to fly out and partake in the beyond moving event that it was. Over those last two weeks the money began to pour in as people came to realize the harsh reality that sarcoma takes lives and the realization of why raising money is so important began to sink in. A total of around $16,000 was raised, which filled my heart with gratitude at a time when I needed to be reminded that I wasn't alone; that people cared and wanted to make a difference. But even more moving for me was watching as student after student and teacher after teacher got up to shave their heads and donate their hair. The momentum was contagious, and teachers had students lining up to call their parents to get permission before taking their place in the hairdresser's chair on the stage in the auditorium. There were over 50 people who participated, who showed that they cared and wanted to make a difference, wanted to help bridge the gap between those with cancer and those without.

There are no words to explain how proud I am of all those who participated, as well as donated, but especially of my two sisters who decided that, while there was nothing they could do to help me or their big brother-in-law, this was a way they could help change the future.

Chapter Nine:
The New Regime

Disclaimer: I am not advocating the use of any of the methods in this chapter for legal reasons. Nor are they meant to diagnosis, treat or cure any illness.

There are no words or way to explain the level of desperation that overcomes you when you realize someone you love more than anything in the world may vanish from your life. As I began to do research on sarcoma and exactly what Cam's prognosis looked like, the impeding dread felt like it would suffocate me at times. I strongly believe in mind over matter, and that we as a society do not understand how powerful our brains are, so it was very important to me that Cam maintain a positive outlook and not give up hope.

In order to support this, I decided very early on to do something I had never done in my relationship with him before and had promised I never would; I began to hide things and at times outright lie to Cam. I would sneak out of bed after he had fallen asleep, unable to sleep myself. I felt desperate, as if the sand was free-falling out of our hour-glass of time together. I would set my laptop up in the kitchen and research various treatment centers, both Western medicine, as well as alternative. I spent hours in different chat rooms searching for someone who had a hopeful story to share and finding none. I would empty Kleenex box after Kleenex box while begging God to not take my best friend. I created files on my computer of all the places we could go, their pros and cons lists, ideas for how to raise money to pay for the expenses, as well as trying to determine what could be done while still living at home. I tried desperately to find out if there was any way I could help; any way I could stop the train that was heading straight towards us. I needed to know that there was not a single rock I did not overturn; that if there was an option, I looked at it and either dismissed it or added it to its corresponding file. And then when the sun would start to come up, and I knew Cam would wake up soon, I would hide the mound of Kleenex in the garbage or flush them in the toilet, turn my computer off and slide back into bed.

Sometimes I would drift off to sleep for a little while and sometimes I would just lay there and watch Cam until he woke. And then I would lie and say I had an okay sleep, a bit restless but fine, while diverting the attention back onto him and what that day held in store for us. It became clear to me that going anywhere outside of Canada for treatment was not going to be an option, and while this was something I, at times gently and at other times forcefully brought up, it was not to manifest. There is no way to know how things may have gone had we chosen to take a different path. And while I still believe that there are other options than what our Western medicine recommends, it was not to be our story. I have had to learn to forgive myself for not pushing harder and forgive others for not being more open to options other than what was offered to us by the doctors here. I've learned to accept we were all scared and desperate; it just manifested in different ways and what we put our belief in contrasted.

I never told Cam about my late-night research sessions; however, a couple of months before he passed away, he was on my computer doing something for me and came across the files. He opened them up out of curiosity and because we had never hidden anything from each other, going on my computer and reading documents was not seen as strange in our relationship. When he asked me about them, he was crying. I fessed up and told him about those early months of his diagnosis when I was trying to come up with as many options and plans as I could. He continued to cry and thanked me for spending so much time trying to save him without ever asking for recognition for all I was doing. The truth is, I never cared about the recognition; all I cared about was getting to keep him.

When I realized that whisking Cam off to some treatment center wasn't going to be an option, I began to increase my research on what could be done from home to either treat or at least stall the cancer growth. From what I found, cancer can only flourish and spread in people with low immune systems. Unfortunately, our world is set up to lower our immune systems, from the food we eat, to the air we breathe and all the electronics constantly interfering with our systems. Sadly, chemo greatly reduces one's immune system and is why there is so much controversy about doing it as many people believe it simply speeds up the process to death. That is for every person to decide on their own, and while I was super against it from all I read, Cam was too scared to not follow his doctor's advice and went forward with it, which I supported because it was his body and life. He began a very intensive regime of going for 8 hours of chemotherapy (Doxorubicin as well as Ifosfamide) three days in a row and then would have two weeks off and come back again on the third week. This made for exhausting days where different family members would take turns sitting with him while he was strapped to a chair or hospital bed and had poison slowly dripped into his arm and body.

Once again, believing in the power of the mind, I would create visualizations for Cam and me of an army of cancer cells rampaging his body and pillaging all his healthy cells. And then in would swoop the poisonous gas designed to seek and destroy those all-so-powerful cancer soldiers. I would continue with the visualization of the poison (chemo) traveling through his body looking for the enemy and destroying it. In reality, we knew that the chemo was also destroying good healthy cells and that it could not differentiate between cancer and healthy cells; however, in our visualizations we opted for the best case scenario where it only went after cancer. At other times, we would talk to the cancer, we would thank it for all that it had taught us, that it had reminded us how very lucky we were to have each other and had made us appreciate every day in a way that I believe you only can when your own mortality, or that of someone who matters more than life itself, is threatened. We would tell the cancer cells all that it had given us, all we had learned and were grateful for and then give it permission to go, that we didn't need its services any longer and would not forget the gifts it gave us. And while this may sound crazy, it was not untrue.

We often spoke about cancer being an incredible opportunity to learn about ourselves and grow in our relationship. And I often said, that as long as Cam survived, I would be grateful for the experience and the slap across the face to stop worrying about all the small day to day things and just be happy in this very moment as it is truly all any of us have. Although he didn't survive, the struggle to hold onto those still very real gifts this experience provided me, continues.

I preferred to be the person who went to chemo with him first thing in the morning and often stayed until after lunch. Partly, it was so I could begin the visualizations and walk him through them, but as time went on he told me that even when I wasn't there he would quietly do them on his own, as it was easier than the terror of being hooked up to IV's with chemo in them and wondering if he was subjecting himself to all of this pain for nothing. I also went because early-on in one of his first treatments I decided that if he had to endure the pain of having a needle poked into his hand, and trying to find a vein that could tolerate being subjected to the IV and chemo, then I sure as hell could watch it.

This, I'm sure, sounds far easier than it ever was. This may not sound like much of a sacrifice. However, a part of me felt like it was dying every time I sat in the chair beside him or on the edge of the bed and let him squeeze my hand with the hand of the arm that was safe from pain that day. I was left feeling powerless every time I watched him grind his teeth, roll his eyes out of pain, or open his mouth while shaking his head violently. He tried desperately not to move his arm with the needle in it, yet every instinct of his was to rip it away.

I quickly learned how to be his advocate. We learned the nurses who could find the vein on the first try 80% of the time and the ones that knew how to do it with minimal pain. We knew the ones that would get their two tries in or who often dug for the vein even though that wasn't allowed. And we knew the ones that left large painful bruises due to puncturing the vein and then putting chemo in anyway. And I became good at requesting our favorite nurses, at warning new ones that his veins look good but would collapse as soon as the needle was put into the skin; at remembering which arm had last been subjected to the treatment, at being firm about the two strikes and you're out if they didn't succeed at getting the IV in. I couldn't stand the idea of Cam going on his own and being his polite self and silently contorting his face in pain while praying they got it right. I needed to be there to witness the pain and try as best I could to limit it.

Looking back on it I don't think I realized how exhausting those hospital visits were for both of us. It was our reality and somehow we just adjusted as best we could. We figured out how to snuggle in the single hospital bed and watch movies. I finished my Masters of Social Work and prepared for my oral defense sitting beside his hospital bed. We decorated gingerbread houses and I finished quilts by hand while we talked for endless hours. At times we would let fear take over and would simply sit as our tears dripped down our faces. I learned to stop wearing makeup in order to avoid black mascara tears streaking my face. We laughed whenever we could and often got strange looks from others. Cam flirted with all the sexy nurses and I began to learn about their lives outside of work. We became almost comfortable with our new life, and the people in it became like family in many senses of the word. Essentially, we accepted that this was the hand we had been given and decided to play it as well as we could.

As I previously mentioned, initially we decided to play fully by the doctor's rules. Cam stopped taking all the vitamins and health supplements that they warned could potentially interact and limit the chemotherapy's effectiveness. We wanted to give it the best shot possible. And, after three months when the results came back with cancer shrinkage, we knew that the chemo was indeed working. Be that as it may, despite our visualizations, it was also working its wonders on all his healthy cells and Cam was feeling weaker and weaker. I remember one day after a treatment, we decided to go for a walk, as they recommended that he still try to get 30 minutes of exercise a day.

So, off we went with our dog Bentley and a Frisbee to the dog park. After about 7-10 minutes of walking, at a pace that would have driven him crazy only months before, Cam laid down in the grass and proceeded to fall asleep. Once again, making the best of a strange situation I played fetch with my dog all around Cam's sleeping body until he awoke nearly an hour later and we walked home. I tell this story as it illustrates how the standard Western cancer treatment of chemotherapy not only required days of our lives to be spent in hospital hooked to an IV, but drained the energy and ability to embrace life as he once had. The final straw for us continuing to blindly listen and follow the doctors was when our honeymoon to Costa Rica was cancelled six days before we were supposed to leave, due to the fact that Cam's white blood cell count was dangerously low. He needed a $2,500 injection in order to help increase his white blood cells and even then travel, especially outside Canada, was not advised. With the knowledge that the chemo on its own was killing the cancer, we decided to see if we could not do something to rebuild and save his healthy cells so that he could begin to enjoy life fully again.

This is where all the research I had been doing on those sleepless nights came into play. While I wish I could reference all the sources that helped us decide what form of supplements Cam should take, unfortunately I did not keep a record of all that I had learned. Prior to writing this chapter, I tried to locate the files I had made full of the research I had done; unfortunately, I have not been able to do so. I sadly assume that when I got a new computer after Cam died that I did not see the need at that time to save the research I had done. I will reference what I can when able in case you wish to read further on this matter (see Appendix Two). This being said, please note that I am not trying to claim to know how to cure cancer or prolong anyone's life. I am simply sharing our journey and the supplements that Cam took based on the research I did.

Cam began to take numerous high-quality vitamins, which included a multivitamin, B-100 complex, 10,000 IU's of vitamin D and fish oils daily. He also had enzymes before every meal to help digest the food and probiotics with his food both in the vitamin form as well as natural food based form. In addition, he would drink fermented kombucha, various tinctures from a Chinese Medicine Doctor to help clean his liver and kidneys, and 4 liters of fresh vegetable juices daily that we would make. Grounding sheets were put on our bed to pull the EMF's from us as we slept, we bought a Water Structuring Unit for our shower, a hand held Water Structuring Unit to use under the tap and eventually a unit for our entire house so that all our water was alive, PH balanced at 9 and free of chemicals and toxins (see Appendix Two). We also became focused on being conscious of our PH balance and eating foods that neutralized it, due to research I had found at that time that showed that cancer flourishes in acidic environments.

If we couldn't find something organic, we simply did not eat it, as our bodies struggle to digest pesticides in general, let alone when compromised. Similarly, we began to avoid sugar or anything that would break down to sugar as there are findings that say that cancer cells prefer to feed off of sugar. This made sense to us due to the fact that, when he would have a PET scan in order to see all of the cancer cells light up on the imaging machine, they would have him drink a special sugar liquid with the explanation that the cancer cells are drawn to it and absorb the sugar, which then glows on the screen. So, if they absorb and are drawn to that sugar, it seems only logical they are also drawn to sugar in our diet.

Essentially, we tried to follow a Paleo diet which eliminates all processed foods. Cam began to take various forms of herbal mushrooms such as chaga, turkey tail, coriolus reishi, shitake among others I no longer remember the names of in pill form, powder, tinctures and teas I would make. I also would brew cat's claw and astragalus root teas for us both to drink even though they tasted worse than I could ever describe. Cam took cumin and turmeric pills due to their anti-cancer fighting properties. Every morning in his vegetable-based protein shake he would add raw maca powder in such large doses we might as well have started snorting the stuff, organic freeze dried moringa oleifera leaf powder, ormus supergreens, flax seed oil, hemp hearts, chia seeds and apple cider vinegar.

In addition to all this, I administered coffee enemas two to four times a day to pull out toxins and reduce pain (see Appendix Two). Cam began to do research into the healing benefits of THC versus CBD in both marijuana plants and then hemp plants. This resulted in him getting his license and us buying all the equipment to have a legal 15 plant grow op in our basement so that he could grow his own plants and ensure the quality was high in CBD's which research has shown to have cancer fighting properties without the high from THC. There were other things we did, and yet I can't seem to remember. Essentially, if I heard it had potential to fight cancer or increase one's immune system, then I would research everything I could about it, and once satisfied, order it. As you can imagine this meant thousands of dollars were spent monthly.

Cam began to work with a Chinese medicine doctor and received acupuncture once a week in order to offset some of the effects of the chemo. We started going to hot yoga three to four times a week and practicing meditation daily. Cam, being a musician, with his main love being drumming was drawn to a drumming circle and began to attend every Friday evening out in the community, where 50-150 people would gather at a community hall to play all kinds of drums and percussion instruments that were provided. Here we could drum as a community, as well as partake in what they called a stress release round, where the lights were turned out and we had the opportunity to hit our drums as hard as we wanted as, well as the chance to simply scream out all of the pain we had inside.

This was my favorite part as there are not many places you can go and simply scream at the very top of your lungs until your voice breaks, and I would start to sob. It was there that we allowed our fear and anger to come to the surface and leave our bodies.

Somehow, through all of this we managed to continue to laugh lots and lots. We would just be silly whenever we could be. I saw it as my mission to make him laugh at least once every day, and Cam still remains the funniest person I have ever met hands down so he always had me laughing even at times through my tears. We realized all too well how much cancer was not fair, it changed our entire day to day life, and stole all kinds of things from us, but it didn't get to steal who we were or our spirit. Bitterness is a choice, one we refused to choose. I saw many people who were given the cancer diagnosis become angry miserable people, but Cam refused to do that because for him life was too beautiful to stop loving every second of it, even if some of those moments were painful and not what he had envisioned.

Within two weeks of beginning all the supplements and taking things into our own hands, he began to have more energy. The following week he had chemo again and rather than being exhausted for days afterwards he found he had the energy to begin going to the gym for two hours nearly every day even after an 8 hour day of chemo. We had been avid hikers and lived close to the Rocky Mountains, and suddenly he had the strength to begin to do hikes again every weekend, even after a full week of chemo treatments. We had our life back, we started to be in control again, rather than cancer being in control. However, while all of this was worth it, it was also exhausting and very time consuming. Eventually, I had to start work and that meant Cam was left to remember all the things he had to take on his own as well as take more of a lead in making the teas. And then the day came that he, too, returned to work, the cancer was in remission, we seemingly had won and now it was time to get life really back to normal. Sadly, there was no possible way to continue the vigorous regime we'd had Cam on while both of us worked full time. We prayed that what we could manage to do would be enough. But it wasn't, and even when we learned that the cancer was back, and back with a vengeance, we did not have the energy to fully return to the extremely strict regime.

I can still taste the anger I felt towards Cam when I, in my matter-a-fact way, announced that everything would be fine because this time we knew exactly what to do to beat his sarcoma. He explained to me, with the same determination, that he did not have the energy to continue that lifestyle in the long term. That he needed to die so that I could get back to living. We yelled and we cried, I begged and at times he agreed, but in the end I had to respect him and his decision. He wanted more than anything to live, but he knew that to be alive is not the same as living. And while we had the energy to maintain our new regime the first time he had cancer, it was with the belief that as long as we got him better then we could relax a bit and go into a maintenance plan that was more structured than the average person, but still allowed us to travel without a spare suitcase filled with our juicer and various pill and tincture bottles.

Learning that this was not so, learning that in order for Cam to survive, in order for us to have more time together, and who knows how long that would have been, he would need to maintain a daily strict lifestyle that would never allow him to work or simply enjoy a pizza, pop and ice cream without worrying about its effects on him, was just too much to bear. And so, our focus painfully changed from curing him to eliminating as much pain as possible and allowing him to live a bit longer and have a high quality of life until the day he decided to leave this earth.

Respecting his choice not to fight, acknowledging that he was right, that I would not have had the vitality to continue in the way we were for years to come was harder than I can ever express. The absolute heart-break of feeling like we had found the cure and yet it was too complicated to enact, too much of a constant burden for us to live with, continuously felt like absolute defeat. I wish with every ounce of my being that he hadn't gotten sick, that when he went into remission it had lasted longer or been permanent, that we had the ability to not need to work and hire people to help us go back to the full regime. But that wasn't our reality. And the longer I am alone and reflect on Cam's and my relationship, the more I am coming to understand why he did not want that life for me. That he saw more than anyone how hard I worked hours before he got up and after going to bed to prepare drinks, teas and tinctures, to take care of him even when he desperately didn't want me too.

In many ways, as he said, he died so that I could live. Not in the literal sense, but so that I could fully enjoy and embrace my life, my dreams. So that the rest of my life was not consumed with calculating PH balances, hospital visits, and the constant awareness that at any time the cancer could come back. Cam didn't want that for me, even if I would have been willing to endure it all, if only it meant I had him. He loved me enough to know that in the end it would ruin me; I would be so exhausted and all consumed by him that there would be nothing left for me and he couldn't stand that thought.

Chapter Ten:
My Miracle

"Today I witnessed a miracle. I held my husband in my arms as he went into cardiac arrest and he died. For an hour I held him and said my goodbyes and all the 'I love yous' I could. And then I held my husband as he came back to life all on his own. Today I witnessed a miracle of life and another day with this man I love so much!"

Elizabeth Leanne Facebook Post January 29, 2014

It had been six weeks since he'd had any seizures. Six weeks of feeling like maybe we had gotten things sorted out, maybe just maybe we would be okay, that his meds would be able to keep the seizures at bay long enough that the natural stuff we both so believed in, could have more of an effect on him. It was January 29, 2014 a day I will never forget. A day that will remain etched in my mind, in my body, in my heart forever. I think I aged a lot that day. I learned more about myself and my ability to love and put my own needs or emotions aside when another needed me. I will forever be changed from this entire experience, but from that day specifically, as it was on that day that my understanding of the thin line we all walk between life and death became glaringly clear. I learned that we are all on borrowed time and that there is no warning for any of us, not really. And I learned that medical doctors, who can explain a lot of things, at times have to simply admit that there is no explanation for what our bodies and spirits can do. I learned that miracles do exist.

We got up like any other morning. It was Wednesday January 29th. I remember thinking that we had pretty much made it through January without needing to go to the hospital and feeling a sense of relief that life was kind of normal. Cam and I had been talking

103

about me returning once again to work in February, and while he wasn't excited about the idea, he understood that I couldn't be off forever. He had been doing so well for the last 3 weeks, I began to feel there really was no excuse for not going back. Cam woke me up at 7:30am asking if we could go to the Chuckwagon Café in Turner Valley, his favorite breakfast joint. I usually said no, as I liked to try to avoid eating out as much as possible, but knew that this response usually ended up in an argument, so I said yes.

Cam had just received a new drug called Voltrient which wasn't covered by health care and cost $4,500 a month out of pocket. Today was the first time he was going to take the pills. There was a lot of hope that this new medication might give him an extra 6-12 months by essentially holding the cancer at bay. Cam fully believed that the medication would get rid of his cancer completely and I never had the heart to tell him this wasn't to be expected. Hope is an amazing thing and it is one thing that Cam never gave up on. This was the one thing that he clung to and he would become furious when I showed any wavering in my level or dedication to hope. Hope had long since eluded me, though I struggled daily to continue to be positive and instill hope in Cam on the days he himself began to waver. The only things I have ever lied to Cam about were that I had been given his prognosis and thus, I no longer believed he would grow old with me, as well as the sleepless nights shortly after his diagnosis when I would research alternatives. Although, honestly I was starting to feel like maybe, just maybe, he was right to be so hopeful and that he was going to be the exception.

I was standing in our en suite bathroom brushing my teeth as Cam sat on the edge of the bed right after taking his medications and vitamins. I heard him yell, "Oh my God! Oh my God!" and thought the new medication was making him dizzy. He had gotten up and was staggering towards me and I yelled with a mouthful of toothpaste, "Well, sit down then!", annoyed that he was trying to walk if dizzy. The next moments are crystal clear in my memory, and yet all blend together at the same time. I saw him fall forward and heard the sound of his face hitting the dresser. I remember running to him thinking he had fainted or tripped, only to realize he was having a seizure and was not breathing. I dropped my toothbrush and consciously told myself to swallow my toothpaste so I could call 911. I still shiver at the memory of the horrible seconds, which felt like they dragged on and on, while I waited for my cell phone to turn on. I vividly remember seeing him take his first breath of air and feeling the sense of relief wash over me. And then, the realization that I needed to move his body as it was blocking our bedroom door from opening, hit me. Somehow I found the strength to lift him from under his arms and drag him out of the way. Later, I would notice that I broke some of my finger nails painfully low in this process; however, the adrenaline pumping through my body in that moment allowed me to remain unaware of this fact at the time.

I carefully listened to 911 and followed their instructions to lock my dogs into a spare bedroom and unlock the front door. I watched as Cam's eyes opened and I realized he was awake; he was alive. I repeatedly told him everything was going to be alright, the paramedics were on their way. These memories and the emotions that accompanied those first 10 minutes still pulse through my mind.

I remember the relief that took over when I realized that the paramedics were here and I was no longer solely responsible for keeping him alive. Finally, I could pass the baton to someone I considered more suited for this job. As I heard them calling out and coming up the stairs, I had the realization that I should put some clothes on and quickly grabbed pants and a sweater without consideration, not even thinking of underwear or a bra. Modesty had been overcome with my desire to protect this man I loved so very much.

At this point he was chatting with the paramedics and they were starting an IV while he sat on the end of the bed. It was then that he went into his second seizure, which was quickly followed by his first cardiac arrest. I stood there feeling frozen, watching them cut his shirt off so they could use the defibrillator, while thinking how sad he would be to lose his favorite shirt, hearing for the first time "I can't get a pulse, he's not breathing", and realizing that he may never get the chance to be upset about his shirt. I stood in the doorway 7 or 8 feet away and watched them lift him from the bed onto the floor and begin CPR. It was as if this wasn't my life, how could this be my life? How could this be Cam? I took what felt like my first breath along with him after learning that he was back, that they had a pulse.

Calmly, I agreed to meet them at the Black Diamond hospital, only five minutes from our home, with the knowledge that STARS helicopter ambulance was on its way to pick him up to take him to the Foothills Hospital in Calgary. I do not remember driving to the hospital. I do not remember if I put my seatbelt on, if I stopped at the stop sign, or if I drove the speed limit. But I do remember parking my car at the hospital while leaving my purse sitting on the seat and running towards the hospital with tears streaming down my face, absolute panic setting into my heart at the fact that I didn't know what may have happened in the few minutes we were apart. A paramedic was waiting and ran with me through the back doors of the hospital into a room where I saw my amazing husband with various kinds of tubes hooked up to him lying on a hospital bed. I was told that in the few minutes we were apart he had had two more seizures and went into cardiac arrest again; however, Cam was revived and breathing on his own.

My heart still breaks for me and for everyone else in the world who has ever had this conversation or ever will with a doctor. I was told by an extraordinarily compassionate doctor, who I will never forget, that Cam would likely never regain consciousness. Then I was asked to make the hardest decision I will hopefully ever make, and one I'd never wish on anyone; to no longer resuscitate him and let him go if he went into another cardiac arrest.

The feeling of terror still pulses through my stomach when I remember talking to Cam's father on the phone, to update him, and seeing the doctor run into Cam's room and out of the one we were standing in, while telling me I had to come now. I hung up the phone without thinking of the panic that would likely cause on the other end and ran towards my husband while hearing the words, "He has gone into cardiac arrest again. We are going to unhook him. Stay with him as long as you like and talk to him, he might still hear you."

With every ounce of my being I wished the doctor was talking to someone else, that this couldn't be my life, not my husband, my love for life who he was speaking of. Looking at the clock and seeing that it was 10:15 am; that three hours prior we had laid in each other's arms in bed completely unaware of what was in store. I laid my head down on his chest while wrapping my right arm around his head. Realizing as I lay there that this was the last time I'd feel his warmth. I gave in and let the tears overtake my body like they were alive all on their own.

While holding Cam, I reminded him of all my favorite moments of us from the last 15 years, and of how lucky I have been to have him in my life, for him to have been the biggest part of my life. I told him that I wouldn't trade any of the memories to escape the pain, how very deeply I love him, that I promised to follow my dreams and never underestimate my potential, even if he wasn't there to keep pushing me; that I forgave him for everything, that it was okay to go now and that I'd be okay and very loved.

I remember saying goodbye, how that word caught in my throat, threatened to choke me. The horrible realization that his feet were turning yellow, and then looking at his hand and seeing that they, too, were taking on a cold yellow color. And then, the shock that my cheek was cold and that the reason my cheek was cold was because there was no warmth left in his chest. And with this, came the realization that nearly destroyed me, that this was the end, he was gone.

At 11:20am, when he started to stir, I thought that it was his body having spasms. The doctor had warned me that at times the body will still twitch or move even after a person has died. When his arms and legs began moving and my aunt and I had to hold him down, I thought, *this is far worse than simply holding his dead corpse, now I have to restrain him.*

I did not realize that I was beginning to witness a miracle, one that would confuse and amaze everyone who heard of it. I remember the fear and hesitant hope when Cam opened his eyes and reached for my head, the glorious pain of him pulling my hair until my face was touching his, the realization that he was actually alive and how survival mode kicked in as I realized he was more scared than I was, and he needed me possibly more than he has ever needed me before. I remember how I rose to the challenge and pushed all my confusion, fear, sadness and joy aside to be with him and his every emotion. In a wave gratitude filled me as I realized that I was given a second chance with him, that I was given what everyone who has ever lost someone wishes for: time. I have never felt more love or protective of anyone or anything then I did in that moment, and for all the moments that followed while he was on this earth. My whole existence became to make Cam comfortable and ensure he was safe. My emotions took on minimal precedence, as I focused on him and his questions.

Seizures often cause memory loss, and it's hard to know what dying and coming back to life can do to a person, since it isn't exactly a regular occurrence. As Cam regained the ability to speak, it quickly became apparent that he had not lost his spunk or goofy attitude. When the nurses asked what he wanted to eat, his response was "pizza", something that made us all laugh as gluten or dairy were not part of his regular diet.

Understandably, Cam had lots of questions and it quickly became apparent his short term memory was being wiped out every four to six minutes and he would start asking the same questions again about why we were in the hospital, which hospital, how much dexamethasone he was on and then be understandably shocked as he learned that he'd had five seizures and had gone into cardiac arrest three times, and that the last time he had brought himself back without any medical assistance.

Cam's oncologist explained to us the next day that there had been a zero percent chance of Cam being resuscitated with a defibrillator due to the progression of his cancer and its locations. And that it was simply unheard of that someone, especially someone in Cam's state, could come back to life after their heart had stopped all on their own. Within the next three days I would hear from seven different doctors that there was no medical explanation for what had happened, that he had undergone miraculous recovery, that he simply was a miracle and that it was not his time. It was humbling to hear all of these very well-educated doctors admit that they had no explanation and were as amazed as everyone else.

Later on the evening of January 29th, Cam was transferred to the Foothills Hospital so he could be under the care of his oncologist. That night in the emergency ward we met with more doctors and they did tons of blood work, a CT of his head which showed no increase in swelling and thus no explanation for the seizures. To everyone's continued surprise, an echocardiogram of his heart showed there was no sign of the two tumors which originally were there. Essentially, Cam was perfectly healthy, other than still having cancer, and there was no explanation for his seizures or going into cardiac arrest. And there was definitely no explanation for how he managed to come back to life 65 minutes after being declared dead.

During the night, one of the doctors asked Cam how he was feeling. Now, knowing Cam as well as I do, his response was not a surprise to me, but the poor doctor who had never met Cam before and had read in the chart all that Cam had endured that day, nearly had a cardiac arrest of his own when Cam swung his legs off the hospital bed and started to do a little jig singing, "I beat death, I beat death", while swinging his bent arms side to side.

And with that Cam's reputation grew even further than it did by simply being the patient who came back to life after an hour. His story was not only about him being a miracle, but also about his absolute love for every second of life and his willingness and ability to make every second count even if on bed rest in a hospital. This touched many staff.

Over the next eight days in hospital, he would fist pound his male nurses and chat about Netflix or music with everyone who would listen. He became protective of his roommate and saw it as his personal job, while in the hospital, to ensure she was getting the care she needed. As a frail 88 year old woman, her body was starting to fail her as was the volume of her voice. When she would call for help, Cam would often end up yelling out what she was asking for as the nurses couldn't hear her on the intercom, or he would call the nurse himself to come and help.

While he couldn't wait to be discharged, we made the best of it and spent 10-15 hours a day snuggled on the hospital bed talking, reading, watching The Adventures of Merlin on Netflix or visiting with friends, family, or hospital staff with a few extra minutes on their hands. There was nowhere else I really wanted to be, every minute felt like stolen or borrowed time and I didn't take a second for granted. I knew I was lucky, that it was all precious. Suddenly every interaction took on a new meaning, new value, and it didn't matter if Cam became frustrated with the situation or grumpy because he was tired or hungry. All that mattered was I was with him, that he was alive.

I will treasure those last 16 days, as they were Cam's gift to me, a gift most never get, but my stubborn man was determined to come back and ensure he had the opportunity to tell me goodbye and specifically instruct me how I was to go on without him. It would not be until he was gone that I realized what a gift those conversations were, that he was freeing me, that he had seen how unimaginable the level of pain would be and he needed to help instruct me how to maneuver it. He gave me the opportunity to say all I needed to say again and to ask all the hard questions we do not like to discuss.

While he remained hopeful that he could still beat cancer to most people, when it was just the two of us, he would speak with an urgency that even at that moment informed me that he knew time was no longer on our side. Cam told me specifically how I was to conduct my life after he was gone; things I was to do as well as what would happen at certain times, much of which seemed impossible. However, many of his predictions have begun to come true in exactly the time frame he outlined. Cam offered me hope without me even realizing it at the time. He offered me hope that it wouldn't always be so painful, I wouldn't always hurt so badly. He gave me permission and, indeed, specific instructions to go on living, and to live well and fully. He set me free and provided time for us to ensure that, when he did leave this earth, there were no words left unsaid, no questions on either side that had not been asked, no regret or guilt about the past or how I was now to continue forward. There is no greater gift we can give the one we love.

Chapter Eleven:
A New Kind Of Love

WARNING: This chapter is sexually explicit and discusses a content you may be uncomfortable reading.

When a symptom first develops, it can be hard to detect its cause. Life is constantly changing and so many things we experience could be explained away or ignored for a time. I remember when I first realized that Cam's sex drive differed from my own. It was a strange realization, one that I questioned, and yet when looking back on the last few weeks realized that he simply wasn't as interested as he had once been. Now there were many factors at play, and even more possible explanations. Some were more palatable then others. This realization came in November 2011.

Possible Explanation One: Up until August 2011 we had been in a largely distant relationship with Cam living in Calgary, Alberta and myself in Victoria, British Columbia. For anyone who has ever been in a long distance relationship there is a sense of urgency when you do get your precious time together and deep longing when apart. For us, this resulted in hours locked in a bedroom, bouts of passion on the living room floor, and much water wasted as a normal shower took on a life of its own. We were crazy about each other and completely obsessed with being touched, kissed, and held. My body came alive at the slightest touch. We often joked that even when we had tried to break up, even when we logically figured we couldn't be together, our physical attraction to each other made it impossible.

We fit together perfectly, were on the exact same vibration level and the chemistry that resulted was mind blowing. So what changed? On my end, nothing. I still grew weak when he walked into a room; still felt every cell turn on when he even lightly touched me, still craved him every second. If anything, my longing and desire only grew. Yet I was experiencing something I had never experienced before: rejection. And not just occasionally, but more often than not I would play games with myself, where I would note the date I had last come onto him and then decide I would wait to see how long it took before he came onto me.

However, inevitably I couldn't help myself and within two to three weeks I would be overcome with desire and try to spark that flame in him. Sometimes it worked, sometimes it didn't. Either way, I was always left wondering why that time he was interested but not the other time.

Possible Explanation Two: As you may remember Cam quit drinking in April 2010. When he seemed to lose interest in our sex life, I did lots of research and found that it was not all that uncommon for people's sex drives to change after getting sober. Cam had told me I was the first person he had had sex with in over five years where he wasn't under the influence. Yet when he was still drinking, he had never had a problem being intimate with me when sober.

Even on our very first night together when he was as nervous as a 13 year old trying to figure out how to put his arm around a girl for the first time, Cam was completely sober. Now it took him longer than I think it normally did but his desire was fully there. He had later said that when he wanted me completely sober and had butterflies trying to make a move he knew he was 'in trouble' and that I was like no one he had ever slept with before. But I hoped that maybe this was just him learning to adjust to always being sober and losing some of the excitement or adventure that he felt more comfortable engaging in when under the influence. So I thought maybe this was it or maybe, just maybe, he was bored with me.

Possible Explanation Three: He simply isn't into me anymore. This was the hardest of the explanations to think of. But it also made sense that if he wasn't attracted to me anymore, he wouldn't be all that interested in sleeping with me. I tried to determine what might have changed to cause this change in his feelings, but couldn't come up with anything. I'd lost weight and looked great, my hair was the same, I hadn't changed the way I acted or dressed, so I thought maybe he just lost interest. I felt desperate to change his mind, entice him and remind him of why he fell in love with me in the first place. But no matter what I did, nothing worked, or if it did, then the next time it wouldn't.

What I hadn't realized until later was how confusing and scary this was for Cam. He later explained to me that he knew he loved me, was still fully attracted to me, and wanted to be with no one else, but just wasn't interested in engaging in sex with me or anyone else. For a young guy who has always been very sexually active, he couldn't understand what was wrong. Eventually we openly talked about all of the three possibilities. He questioned if he had simply grew bored of me, if maybe he wasn't actually attracted to me. We even got counselling to try and revive the spark that was still strong in me but absent in Cam. Eventually we settled on the fact that maybe Cam had just got all his adventurous sexual activity over with at a young age and that his sex drive was taking a break. We also wondered if mine was simply increasing as I got closer to 30.

The one thing that we both easily agreed upon was that when we were both in the mood, the intensity and level of passion was indescribable. We were consumed by the other's presence. Being with him always was like nothing I had ever experienced before. On one occasion when we were discussing our struggling sex life, Cam said that he was confused because he felt like every time we had sex it was better and better, that he had never been with someone he was so comfortable with and who knew exactly what to do and when to do it. We were fully in sync. And yet he marveled that, even though he knew it only kept getting better, as soon as it was over, the desire was gone for a few weeks.

None of it made any sense and left us both confused. Cam offered me an out during this time. He knew I was not sexually satisfied and that feeling desirable was important to me. We talked about ending the relationship as it was becoming apparent that this was not simply a passing phase. However, as always, I questioned what I could live with and knew without a doubt that I would be much happier occasionally having sex but always having Cam than I would be having sex regularly but with another person. And so we began to work on creating intimacy in other ways, of accepting and being grateful for all we did have in our relationship and learning that while sex is often the way we show attraction or affection for those we care about, there are 100's of other ways to do just that.

We never made the connection between Cam's sex drive and cancer when he got diagnosed. The pain in his bones had made things particularly difficult in previous months and chemo sure didn't induce the feeling of sexiness for Cam. He also explained that at times he felt that sex was pointless because chemo had caused him to be infertile and his greatest desire was to get me pregnant and have a family. Without this possibility, the joy and 'risk' of having sex was dampened. By this time our focus had changed and our lack of sex life was no longer of particular concern to either of us. Keeping Cam alive and enjoying every minute became the only focus. So you can only imagine the shock and complete pleasure when suddenly Cam came onto me twice in one week. And my continued delight when the next week was no different.

Shortly after in May 2013, we learned that there were no active cancer cells left in Cam's body. We had done it! There were no words to describe that feeling, the absolute joy that filled us. And then we put two and two together. Cam's sex drive had started to diminish a month before his bone pain started, and it came back two weeks before we learned that the cancer was inactive. The relief we both felt at understanding what had been going on and that it was over was indescribable. We marveled at how lucky we were, how lucky to finally match and work together in perfect unison. Sadly, this reprieve was short lasted.

Looking back, I'm happy I didn't know it was the last time we would have sex, the last time I would feel completely absorbed by our love for each other. August 18, 2013; there was nothing special about it, just simply one of those nights that we crawled into bed and I felt his hands reaching for me; felt myself begin to instinctively respond and shiver. Just another incredible night, where his only concern and focus was on consuming me and ensuring that I felt my body break open, explode, and quiver over and over. From August 23rd till the 28th we went camping in Waterton, BC. There is no word other than 'amazing' to describe that trip. We hiked 59km with both of our dogs, Bentley and Mickey, in three days and took pleasure in having nothing else planned, no agenda.

In those five days I came onto Cam twice but we were staying in a tent and had the dogs with us. Both times Cam said that he didn't trust me to be quiet enough to not traumatize the surrounding campers, many of whom were children. I understood his reasons and although I pouted, agreed he was probably right. By the second week of September, I was starting to get worried. He had shown no interest in me and got angry any time I came onto him. Later, he explained that he also feared that his sudden lack of sex drive meant that the cancer had returned but didn't want to voice such a thing. We fought about sex constantly for two weeks. I was terrified that it might mean the cancer was back, but also began to question whether it had nothing to do with cancer and really had been me all along. He was all I wanted, I craved him and felt that I was going crazy lying in bed next to him every night without being able to have him. I just didn't understand what had happened, didn't want to understand.

116

By the third week of September, I called and spoke with his family doctor. I explained the different symptoms I was seeing and that, for me, the other symptoms paired with his quick lack of libido signified that the cancer was back. Sadly, I was right.

What little sexual interest Cam still had was quickly destroyed by his full brain radiation. No longer was he simply not interested in sex, but he no longer could get an erection. He sadly marveled at the fact that not only was it impossible to keep him stimulated for more than a couple minutes, and even at that it wasn't a full erection, but that he no longer even got 'morning wood'. While beyond heartbreaking, there was an aspect of relief since, without a doubt, I knew it was not me, I was never the problem. Cam was desperate to solve the problem and this time around he quickly reverted back into finding other ways to tell me how attracted he was to me, how much he loved me. My heart repeatedly broke as he spoke about how he felt like a failure as a husband because he couldn't even pleasure me. At first, we tried to find things that might excite him, but this only grew more discouraging.

In Mexico, in November, we purchased Cialis and were giddy with excitement to have hopefully found a way around his inactive libido. Cialis was explained to us to not only activate the blood flow to the penis but also increase arousal in the brain. Both of these were needed if either of us were to enjoy ourselves since having sex while Cam was not in the mood was out of the question for me. Sadly, it did not have the desired effects and that night, which was supposed to be celebratory, ended for us both in tears.

We slowly began to realize that we may never have sex again; however, it wasn't until December that this was confirmed when Cam went to his family doctor to ask if there was anything he could do. He was told that short of getting an injection, or pushing a small pill into the hole of his penis, both of which would force blood to his penis, there was nothing that would ever give him an erection again. Neither of these options would increase his desire to have sex and certainly were not options in our mind.

Dexamethasone, a steroid Cam was on in order to decrease the swelling in his brain, caused his face and stomach to swell. It also eats away at your major muscles and, as a result, his legs and arms shrunk in size. He barely looked like himself. I am still not sure if it was these physical changes that caused the unexplainable to happen, but I began to lose my sexual attraction to him. Part of me wonders if I was trying to protect myself and that constantly wanting something I knew I would never have again became too painful, so I just shut down my libido. Not only did my attraction to Cam decrease, but I no longer found others interesting or had any interest in sex.

While strange, it made our last few months together much easier for me. And my love, compassion, and devotion only grew in intensity. I began to feel protective over Cam, as if he was more my child than husband. I loved him more fiercely than I ever knew was possible. My only concern was his comfort, alleviating pain, trying to prolong his life, and looking for countless ways to bring joy to each of his days. He had always been my everything, but suddenly he mattered more than anything and there was nothing I wouldn't do for him. I had always assumed that in order for a relationship to be truly healthy, the sex life also had to be healthy.

Now I know this isn't the case. I know it is possible to live and fully love and be devoted to your best friend with absolutely no need for physical gratification. Holding each other's hand, a kiss on the top of the head, a strong hug or laying together on the couch or in bed became more meaningful than I knew was possible, more satisfying than any of our sexual encounters ever had been. Simply being in his presence was enough for me, and it was enough for him to be in mine. We became one; we had the strongest friendship and love I could have imagined. It was completely unselfish love.

Chapter Twelve:
The Final Goodbye

On Sunday, February 9th, Cam began to deteriorate. He went from still fully embracing life, having his sense of humor, and being fully present in the moment, to being exhausted. His presence in this world suddenly became less frequent. He had re-started a new drug, Voltrient, on Wednesday the 5th and fatigue was to be expected. However, when he slept for about 20 hours on Sunday, I began to question whether the potential benefits of the drug actually outweighed the drastic decrease in quality of life. I prayed it was temporary and that he would rally, as he had so many times before. I cried wrenching sobs as I watched him on the baby monitor we had set up, while he slept upstairs in our bedroom. I remember the first time the doctor mentioned 'quality of life' and how that phrase made me feel like I was going to throw up right there in the oncologist's office. It was in that moment that I fully realized they had no belief that he would get better, that they were not trying to cure him; only add time to his life and that they had given up hope.

However, by February 2014, I had come to share the doctors' view and saw Cam's quality of life as being of more importance than anything else. In fact, I had made it my personal mission, my full-time job and sole purpose to ensure that his quality of life was as high as it could be. I had tried with all my might to save him. I had done the research and read the books, looked into medical and alternative treatment centers around the world. I had searched for remedies we could order or find here in Calgary and gladly handed over piles of money to ensure he had everything that I had found might possibly do some good. I had cradled him while he cried, sought new and exciting things for us to do together, even as his mobility began to decrease.

My focus was Cam and ensuring that every single day there was something that would bring a smile to his face, bring him some peace and create a memory to hold onto. Only waking to be fed in bed or offered a drink and then falling right back to sleep is not quality of life, it is not really living. And suddenly, I had no idea what to do, no idea how to create quality of life when he could barely stay awake. On Monday, February 10th , we met his oncologist and I voiced my concerns along with the fact that Cam was getting intense headaches again, feeling dizzy when he stood or sat up, was experiencing a dulling of his ears where it was hard to hear, blurry vision, sore ribs, and nose bleeds that were full of massive blood clots.

The doctor decided to cut the dose in half so that the side effects wouldn't be so intense; both of us were relieved by this decision. However, the following morning he was just as tired. There would be moments or, at times, a couple of hours where I saw his sense of humor shine through; however, I never did see him regain his full presence in life.

Wednesday, February 12, 2014, 6pm. I still can hear him scream my name as I filled our water bottles. Still remember running to the bottom of the stairs and yelling up to him, only to hear the smash, which I knew meant he had fallen out of bed. It meant something was horribly wrong. I still remember the feeling of the shot of adrenaline that allowed me to fly up the stairs faster than I knew possible. I found him face down on the bedroom floor seizing and smashing his face into the floor repeatedly, blood running from his nose and the cuts on his head, where he must have hit it as he fell.

The next few minutes and hours flash through my mind like a movie I've watched too many times. Grabbing my phone and dialing 911, crouching beside his body waiting for the seizure to stop. Rolling him onto his side and telling the 911 operator that he has a history of going into cardiac arrest shortly after having a seizure. Cam waking and being confused. Him trying to push me off of him and trying to stand up. Cam finally listening to me and lying down. My beloved crying over and over how scared he was.

I remember my determination to soothe him and validate all he felt at the same time. Cam explaining to me that he had been taking his pulse and he felt it stop, which is why he screamed my name. He went on and on about how scary it was to actually feel his pulse just stop. Once again, we went to the hospital in an ambulance only to find out everything looked fine. The doctor told us we could go home after only two hours. It was just a seizure, nothing more; nothing to panic over.

I marveled at this amazing man I had been blessed to know, love, treasure, touch and share my life and home with. The realization that this might become a more regular part of my life began to sink in and I forced away the ever-growing sense of exhaustion and dread. Not knowing if I should be fearful that he had a seizure exactly two weeks after he had five seizures and three cardiac arrests, or if I should be hopeful that it was the least severe of all the seizures he had had. That maybe they were getting better. Deciding that I would simply be happy he was okay and that we didn't have to spend another night in emergency. We were happy to be in our bed and home together just as it should be.

I often confused love for Cam and the need to be solely responsible for his care. I wanted to be the one to do everything and felt extremely possessive and protective of him. Yet this attempt to keep others at bay and allow me to take care of him meant that I became more and more exhausted as the days turned into weeks and months. In truth, I didn't trust anyone to take care of him the way I knew I could and was doing. The regime he was on for eating, doing enemas, and basically living, was one that many people did not understand or necessarily agree with. Yet I knew it worked, I saw the repercussions when he had a 'small' 'harmless' treat.

Cam also knew how food not in the regime made him feel; however, he struggled, like many of us do, with temptation. When I wasn't there to monitor, Cam often gave into those temptations. When I realized that he likely did not have long to live, I struggled with encouraging him to eat and do anything he wanted and to just 'enjoy life'. Yet, as things progressed and his body became more sensitive, it became obvious that allowing his taste buds to enjoy life often meant the rest of the day and possibly even the next would be painful for him. So, I became okay with being the strict bitch who tried to 'control' him as long as it meant he wasn't in pain.

I didn't need people to understand why I did what I did, or said the things I would to him when trying to discourage a choice he was about to make. Cam knew, and when the temptation passed, always thanked me. His gratitude, love and ability to enjoy life with me was the only payment I needed. Making it harder to accept help from others was the fact that Cam did not want anyone but me to take care of him. He understood I couldn't go on doing it on my own, but feared being left with others. Cam explained to me after he died and came back to life in January, that it was me who was there every time something went wrong; that each time he was okay, he was still alive and that maybe it was because of me, that perhaps someone else wouldn't do the same things and he would die.

I couldn't argue with this, not really. I had to acknowledge that this was a possibility, but reminded him that we couldn't be held captive by this fear. I had to do a lot of my own private work with my therapist and in my heart by acknowledging and trying to come to terms with the fact that he could die every time I left him, and that somehow I would have to find it in me not to blame whoever was left with him for that. I prayed silently that if he died, I was the one there so that I wouldn't struggle with resentment, question what they had done wrong or blame myself for leaving him. I knew I would do everything in my power to keep him alive, and Cam knew this as well. He trusted me more than anyone, as I had been tested and proved myself to him on more than one occasion.

In no uncertain terms, he trusted me with his life and that is an honor I will forever be grateful for. But it had gotten to the point where I knew that if I didn't begin to accept help, I wouldn't be able to keep going or at least not with the same compassion I normally felt. I was exhausted. I was beginning to feel resentment, not so much towards Cam, but towards the situation, towards cancer. I was 29 and a full time caregiver to my 28 year old deteriorating husband. While on some days I felt honored to be so closely linked to this experience, and there was never a day I would have thought of leaving him, there were starting to be days that I resented no longer having freedom to make plans without having to find someone to stay with Cam.

I was thus apprehensive to leave Cam with his mom on Thursday the 13th, so that I could get my tattoo finished. I reassured myself that nothing was likely to happen, and reminded myself that I needed to learn to trust others and that they all loved him and would do anything in their power to also keep him alive. My six butterflies turned out beautiful, more perfect then I could have ever imagined and I was so happy that Cam was going to be able to see them. Cam was beyond amazed when I did show him and thought they looked amazing, which they do. I was excited to post a picture of my fresh vibrant tattoos on Facebook with the following passage,

> *"A butterfly is delicate and beautiful. Yet it must travel far and withstand many trials and transformation before taking on the form for which it is admired. Similarly, Cam and my journey has been one of struggle, transformation, and ultimately a love so beautiful it transcends time and space. Butterflies have always been symbolic to me; however, my love for them grew over the last couple years. It was for this reason rather than simply choosing two colors for our wedding I chose butterflies as the theme. With this meaning and their constant reminder of our vows 'in sickness and health', as well as all the amazing day encompassed, I had butterflies tattooed across my back in all the colors of our bridal party young and old."*

My six butterflies, the number not chosen by me. It was simply the number of wings this skin of mine could hold. And then I realized with awe and a pang of sadness, that this was our sixth year together, a butterfly for every year. I realized if this coincidence held true, then we would not see another year together. What I did not realize was that we would not see another year. Instead, we would only have one more day. The true significance of this beautiful number is still revealing itself to me.

Nearly three weeks after Cam passed, I was at my massage therapist for the first time in a few months. She inquired about the reason behind the six butterflies and when I explained that consciously there had been none, but now realize that is the number of years we were together, she explained that in Numerology the number six means "The Lovers." Tears sprung to my eyes and rolled down my cheeks for there is no better way to describe us. Later that night, I added the numbers of the date he died together which is another practice in Numerology and realized that when 2 (February) is added to 1 and 5 (for 15th), and then 2,0,1,4 are added you get 15 and when 1 and 5 are added you get 6. He left this earth on the day of "The Lovers". My understanding of the significance of all this only grew when my massage therapist sent me the explanation of "The Lovers" card from Osho Zen Tarot Cards (See Appendix Three).

When I returned to Cam's mom's home, I learned that he had slept most of the day, which was not surprising to me. I remember looking at his two water bottles sitting where I had left them hours earlier, still full. To the average person this might not seem so alarming, but to me this signified that things had turned and all I felt was fear as I asked him if he had filled them up. Cam explained that he hadn't drank or ate anything because he just felt so full even though he knew he couldn't be. I started to feel better when at supper that night he had a healthy portion and managed to drink some of his water. That night while Cam napped, I read the pamphlets Home Care had given me on what to expect when someone is dying in the home. I remember my relief when he didn't match all the criteria to look out for.

February 14, 2014, Valentine's Day, was the first time I had 3 hours of organized respite that wasn't a family member. I drove to Calgary and bought big helium heart balloons to add to our already completely decorated house in preparation for the Valentine's Day party we were planning for the 16th. It was a beautiful sunny day and I felt happy, felt like it was going to be okay, like this was sustainable. However, when I came home and relieved the respite worker, I realized that things were progressing faster than I had thought. I realized that he now met the criteria, that if this book was right, he likely did not have much time left.

The respite worker explained she had been unable to get him to drink anything, he had not gone to the washroom, as well as discussed his struggle to remain awake. She stated that when awake, he was quite confused and made little sense. Once again, he hadn't been interested in eating or drinking for me. However, the respite worker told me she was able to get him to eat a bit of soup. After she left, Cam explained that he had had an out of body experience, where he became confused about where he was and couldn't figure out how to get back into his body. He was understandably shaken up by this, though I tried to spin it as being very cool and a once in a lifetime experience in order to calm him.

Yet this greatly concerned me, possibly even more than his lack of interest in food or water. I had watched him over the last few days leaving this world behind. I had watched as he slipped further away, as the color disappeared from his eyes and was replaced by a glassy stare. I knew there was nothing I could do to stop this process. I believe that at times our spirits take test runs at leaving our bodies, particularly as we get close to making this final transition. This belief comes from having spoken to many others who were honored to witness their loved one making their final transition from this world and their recollections of that experience. It is extremely common for palliative patients to discuss visits from loved ones who are passed, to see or experience things others cannot, or to feel themselves leave their body prior to dying.

The fact that he had felt he left his body and couldn't get back in it, the fact that this happened when he was awake and simply seemed confused to others, signified to me that the barrier between this world and the next was growing thin. I texted my mom my heart wrenching realization that I didn't think Cam would last longer than a week. I remember being happy we were having a Valentine's party in two days so that all his friends could have a fun relaxed way to see him one final time. I knew he didn't want to be in hospital, didn't want to have a stream of visitors come in to cry and say their goodbyes. I knew he wouldn't want people to know how close to death he was, as it would likely alter the way they interacted with him and that would have hurt too much to bear.

The next events still play through my head over and over. I've realized I will never know whether he would have lived a few more days or even weeks had things gone differently; that I'll never know or understand why everything happened exactly as it did.

At 3pm, I went up to our bedroom and grabbed his pill case for the day, the one that had each dose of pills in a different compartment; one that was meant to allow Cam some independence with taking his meds. I put them in their compartments, I ensured the right doses went where needed and Cam ensured he took them when I told him it was time. This is how we had worked for the last couple months and it had never been a problem. I had no reason to think that he wouldn't take his medications or that he might miss them. I know this and I remind myself of this whenever I wonder if things would have been different if that morning, when he took his meds, had I just checked the container to be sure. But I had never done this before, never had a reason.

In the morning compartment lay two of his anti-seizure medications. He was supposed to have them at 8am, it was now

3pm. When I questioned Cam on this, he seemed as shocked as I was and swore that he had taken them all, and yet the evidence lay in the container that he hadn't, that somehow they had jammed and not fallen into his hand. I quickly gave them to him along with the medication he was to have at 3pm, and prayed that he would be fine. Cam quickly fell back asleep, it was the only reprieve he got from his horrible headaches on that day. I watched him over the next hour, sleep for 10-15 minutes, and then his face would start to contort and moments later he would wake up crying holding his head between his hands.

This heartbreaking unbearable pain would last for about 5 minutes and then just as quickly disappear, allowing him to fall back asleep for a little while longer. Just before 4pm, Cam woke again crying and yet this time sweat started to drip down his face and when I asked if he was going to throw up, he replied, "Yes." Within seconds of handing him our large blue kitchen mixing bowl, he began to throw up what little soup he had had and lots of bile. Suddenly, I realized he may have thrown up his medications, that an hour may not have been long enough to have them absorb. My initial thought was that I would just give him more and then I realized that this was not something I should decide on my own.

I am grateful for that decision, for had I chosen to give him more meds, and he had still passed away, I would have forever questioned that decision. As luck would have it, Cam's oncologist called to let me know that he had not received Cam's blood test results yet and thus did not know Cam's Dilantin levels; however, someone would call me the next day to advise what should be done if anything. When I relayed all that had happened so far that day, the doctor advised that I give Cam his evening dose of anti-seizure meds early that night but not to re-give the already late dose as it was impossible to know how much he had absorbed before throwing up.

We had dinner reservations for 6 pm at a restaurant in Okotoks called Heartland and by 5pm I called and canceled, as I realized that there was no way Cam could get dressed up in the outfit I had laid on the bed for him that morning. Cam felt horrible and kept apologizing for 'ruining' Valentine's Day, to which I reminded him that all that mattered was being with him, and I couldn't think of a more perfect way to spend this day of love than with him in our home. He promised we would get dressed up another night and go to Heartland to make up for it. Instead, we ordered Chinese food and since I didn't think he would be eating, I even got ginger beef, which was normally a no-no due to the gluten.

My uncle kindly went and picked it all up for us and delivered to our door, as we couldn't leave the house to get it. He even came in and took some pictures of us snuggled on the couch. I posted some of the pictures on Facebook for everyone to see how amazingly magical and perfect our Valentine's Day had turned out with the caption,

> "Well dresses, high heels and dinner reservations have nothing on curling up in pajamas, eating take-out that my uncle so kindly delivered, as we can't leave the house, and enjoying the fireplace and all our Valentine's decorations! We've got each other so this Valentine's Day has been a success even if we had to cancel all our original plans!"

Cam completely surprised me, as shortly after 6pm he started to feel better, much better. Better than I had seen him since the previous Saturday. He fully rallied, and looking back likely used all the energy he had left to make it a perfect Valentine's Day. Little did I realize that often people will have a surge of energy prior to dying. He ate two large plates of Chinese food, drank a liter of green juice and was fully engaged with his sense of humor completely present. I began to think that I had overreacted earlier and that he was fine, just had been feeling off, maybe had a bug, but would be fine now.

After an amazing dinner, Cam pointed to the lights in our living room and told me never to touch the running rod when they are on, that the entire fixture would be conductive. I asked how they cannot have a warning on it, if it could be that dangerous and Cam laughed that he was my personal warning. I did not know at the time that this was the last bit of protective advice he would give me, and now I treasure it. We went downstairs to watch The Adventures of Merlin on Netflix and snuggled together all night, holding hands and loving every second of it. I'm so very happy that I didn't know it was our last night; that really it was like any other night with this man who made my heart swell. We were always just so happy to be in each other's presence, so fully in love and this night was no different.

At 11:25 pm, as we crawled into bed, I nagged him to brush his teeth, as he hadn't in a couple of days. But he was tired and brushing his teeth took effort, which he didn't always have. So I snuggled into his arms and let it go, turning off the light. As we lay there wrapped in each other's arms, Cam said, "You know why I keep coming back and won't die?" I started to laugh thinking about how stubborn he is and that not even death is the boss of him. I asked him why. Cam's response, which I'll treasure forever, was, "Cause I just love you too darn much to leave you alone. I don't want to just die. I keep just falling down without any warning and dying and that's not what I want. I want to get the chance to say goodbye to you." I then asked what he would say if he got the chance to say goodbye to me, and Cam told me how much he loved me, how grateful he was to have had me in his life, and all that he wanted for me, for my life.

As he spoke with tears welling in my eyes, I thought that I would have to get him to repeat some of the things the next day so I could video record it and thus have it forever. When he finished, I said, "There, you got to say goodbye and now you'll have no regrets. We both fully know where the other stands. I love you." He told me he loved me too and we fell asleep in each other's arms completely content, completely in love.

I woke up with a surge of fear, dread and adrenaline. I knew something was wrong even as I said his name quietly the first time, and then loudly the second. As I jumped out of bed and flicked the bedroom light on, I yelled his name for a third time. On the bed lay my beautiful husband not breathing, eyes open. It was 12:01am on February 15, 2014. He waited till Valentine's Day was over. I still have no idea what woke me up. Maybe I felt him stop breathing. Maybe we were so connected that I felt him leave his body, felt the change in his energetic field which was so closely linked to my own.

I stood there staring at him as I realized that tonight was different than all the times before, that he was not having a seizure, he simply was not breathing. Standing there, I wondered for a split second if I should just allow him to go peacefully like this rather than asking his body to go through more. So many of us wish to die in our own bed next to a loved one, and here this wish had become a reality. I could simply do nothing and allow this to be his end. Yet my promise to him, to keep trying and that I must fight just as hard for his life as he was fighting for it, came back to me. The next moments are a blur and yet crystal clear; taking a breath and calling 911, hooking up the defibrillator to his chest, hearing him take a breath, pushing him off the bed to start CPR at the 911 personal instruction. Realizing the front door was locked and I was naked. Not really caring who saw me; my only concern was letting the paramedics in and praying they could be of more use then I felt I was. Watching Cam have his first seizure. My dogs locked in a room throwing themselves at the door, terrified at the fact that their quiet house was suddenly full of commotion and they couldn't protect their owners. Hearing the commotion in the back of the ambulance and realizing he had gone into cardiac arrest, thinking that this might be it. Calling his dad and telling him to come now.

The minutes turned into hours, they dragged on and replayed in slow motion and yet went by in a flash. I remember his roars as his body seized over and over again. A continuous cycle of seizures and cardiac arrests. I stood helplessly watching his body contort and seize, yet was comforted by the knowledge that as long as he was having a seizure, he was alive. And then, without warning, he would become completely still, peaceful even. But it was in these quiet moments that I knew he was dying, he was leaving me. Each of these states were no worse or heartbreaking than the next, just different. For about 20 minutes straight his body didn't have a break between seizures and cardiac arrest; one would lead into the other.

I sat and watched his body contort and pull against the restraints that had been applied to keep him on the hospital bed and protect himself from further injury, then watched him die and go limp, only to either suddenly start seizing again or have him shocked and his arms lift off as the jolt of electricity shot through him. I tried to wade through my terror and listen to the paramedics, nurses and doctor as they marveled at the fact that most of the time when Cam would go into cardiac arrest they would be charging up the machine, and then before they could apply the shock he would get a heart rate back. They formulated various hypotheses for what was happening. I listened to them try to figure out how to stop the seizures, as they appeared to trigger his cardiac arrests. Yet nothing they did seemed to work. I stood helplessly as various drugs were injected or slowly dripped into his IV, the names of such drugs I agreed to without fully hearing them, only hoping that something would work and break the cycle; desperately wanting to believe they had the 'cure'.

At various points, the doctor would ask me again how much more did I want them to do, how far did I want this to go. All I wanted, all I ever wanted was for my amazing husband to get better, to grow old with me, and yet I knew with a certainty I have never experienced before that that would not happen; not in this lifetime. Nonetheless, I did not know how to utter those words, was terrified others would blame me for letting him go, wondered how I had the right to decide when it had gone far enough. The doctor explained to me that the amount of drugs Cam had been given to try to stop the seizures were going to soon likely stop his ability to breath on his own.

Once again, I was asked how I would like them to proceed, listening to my options, none of which were at all appealing. The doctor explaining that things were going to get a lot more invasive for my husband and how far did I want to go? The question I had quickly hated being asked, a responsibility I would never wish on anyone and yet I knew it had to be my decision, I owed Cam enough to not shrink back at this crucial moment. The words that finally gave me my answer; "There is the potential that every time we shock him he feels pain."

I decided that he had fought hard enough, I had fought hard enough and it was time to let go. I could not tolerate to think of him in pain and my absolute devastation and fear of losing him was overridden by my need to protect him in these final moments. Letting him go was my final gift to him; it was the only thing left to do.

I learned later that he had been shocked 14 times and successfully came back each time, and the rest of the time Cam had managed to bring himself back miraculously. That, once again, no one had seen someone do what Cam did that night, that he left everyone confused and questioning all they had been taught. His father and I stood beside him as he went into another cardiac arrest yet again, and I watched the screen as the line ran flat. The sudden realization that it was over as I stood holding him while tears overtook my body. Yet true to Cam's nature, a minute later he got a heartbeat back. I remember feeling like suddenly I was taking my first breath with him at that time, as if I had stopped breathing when his heart stopped beating. For over three hours he had struggled between seizures and cardiac arrest and now he just lay there breathing on his own, with a heart rate of 85, a healthy blood pressure and an ECG that showed nothing to be concerned about.

It was as if he knew that no one was going to try to keep him alive any longer and he just relaxed. He was tired, he was tired of trying to live and live so fully. He did not want to slowly die; he did not want to become bed-ridden or have anyone other than me care for him; he did not want to be in a hospital or hospice. That was not how he wanted to die. That was not how he wanted us to remember him.

The doctor began talking about the possibility that he might pull through the night, but would likely not wake up for many hours due to the amount of medication in his system. I remember the doctor explaining to me it was important to keep his eyes closed so they didn't dry out. This became a focus for me, my job and duty for my darling husband. Finally, I had something I could do for him, I had a way to help other than hold his hand and talk to him, which somehow did not feel enough. This was not as easy as I had originally thought, or as it sounds now. I had to hold my hand constantly over his eyes to keep the lids closed as they kept sliding open.

At one point I allowed them to open for a few moments and stared into the eyes that had mesmerized me from the moment I first saw them. The eyes which are exactly the same hazel color as mine. The eyes we always said our children would inevitably inherit. I wanted to memorize them and yet there was no life looking out of them because Cam was no longer staring back at me. There is no way to describe the emptiness of eyes once a soul has begun to leave the body. No emotion; just vacant glass-like balls. They are not the eyes I wish to memorize, not the eyes which always looked at me with such adoration.

I had explained to Cam at various points that his dad and I were there, that his mom and sisters were on their way. I held him and reminisced my favorite memories of us, told him how proud I was of him and how much I loved him. I thanked him for fighting so hard to live with me and for showing me what real love looked and felt like. When they arrived, I told him that everyone was here now, that it was okay, we would be okay in time and that he could go now, that he didn't need to keep fighting. Two minutes later he went from a heart rate of 85 and perfectly healthy vitals to a heart rate of 296 and died at 3:42am on February 15, 2014.

I stayed with him and watched as a deep purple color creeped up his neck, ears and across his face. I knew that this time he really was gone, but I needed to make sure. I had promised him after he came back on January 29th that I would ensure he truly was dead before I let them cremate him, and I was not going to walk away from my final promise to him.

I unclasped the necklaces he wore and tucked them in my pocket for safe keeping. As I held his hand that bore his wedding ring, I sobbed and remembered the day I put the ring on his finger. My mind was flooded with memories of us laughing, kissing, hugging, of the look on his face when he first saw me walking down the aisle; of just how happy and in love we were. I remembered the vows we made to each other and how we had lived up to them more than I could have ever understood on that day. I had no concept of the compassion, love and devotion that would be required to fulfill them, and yet I accepted and repeatedly stepped up to the challenge without hesitation.

I kissed his hand and thanked him for being the most incredible husband I could have ever asked for, thanked him for making me so very happy and for teaching me that I am worthy of love. And then, with a vow to always love him, but not let my love for him and sadness over losing him hold me back from loving again and living my life to the fullest of my potential, I removed his wedding band from his finger. I stood and bent forward kissing the love of my life, my best friend and the person who I wanted so badly to grow old with on the lips for the last time. I wiped a tear that landed on his face, while muttering, "I told you that you should have brushed your teeth before bed" due to the film that was covering his teeth. The nurse struggled to suppress a laugh, surprised at my remark. Tears ran down my face but I wore a half smile at the fact that even in death he couldn't escape my bossy nattering. I told him I loved him and walking out of the room, going home for the first time without him.

Bentley on December 11, 2011 the day Cam and Elizabeth brought him home on their 3rd anniversary.

Cam on the fishing trip with his dad in July 2012 days before being diagnosed with cancer. You can see the lump on the right side of his neck.

September 2, 2012 wedding cake

**Dream come true Cam and Elizabeth
got married! September 2, 2012**

September 3, 2012 hair began falling out so they shaved it

The view from Cam and Elizabeth's backyard in their new home

Bentley and Elizabeth outside Jasper on the way to their wedding in British Columbia

June 29, 2013 Butterfly Wedding

Cam and Elizabeth's beautiful pedicures

Butterfly Bridesmaids and Flower Girls

Groomsman ties in the colors of each bridesmaid dress

Cam and Mickey

Naked In Solidarity

September 22, 2013

Mexico November 3 – 10, 2013

The day before Cam began to throw up and lost the ability to walk without help

December 11, 2013 celebrating our 5th anniversary in Canmore
on an one horse open sleigh

Christmas 2013 days after Cam was discharged from
the hospital after having his first set of seizures.
Cam wearing his Christmas sweater Elizabeth unbuttoned
before the ambulance arrived and paramedics cut it off.

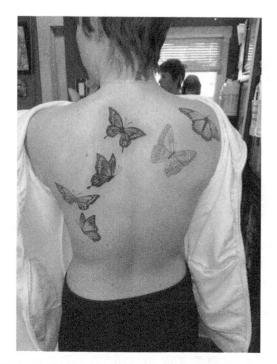

February 13, 2014 Six beautiful butterflies

**February 14, 2014 Valentines Day,
a few hours before Cam had his first cardiac arrest
that evening and lost consciousness prior to dying.**

Cam enjoying his last meal of Chinese food

Elizabeth and Cam's last picture together prior to watching Netflix and then going to bed happy and in love.

Chapter Thirteen:
Living Without Him

I knew that it would be hard to be without him. I knew that the world would seem empty, and that I would have more time on my hands than I knew what to do with. But I had no idea that the world would suddenly feel uninhabitable. That the air would feel toxic to my lungs; that living and breathing would be painful and feel like they were no longer necessary but, in actuality, detrimental to my wellbeing.

Everything suddenly lost its color. Even food became the enemy, getting dry and pasty in my mouth. Sucking all moisture from me and refusing to be swallowed. Instead my stomach revolted against me, and much of my energy those first six days were spent trying not to throw up, trying to keep the gagging to a minimum and popping anti-nausea pills every few hours to take the edge off.

It wasn't simply the loss of Cam I had to adjust to. No, it was as if everything I knew and was familiar with was gone, changed. Things I had taken for granted without even knowing it suddenly were a struggle. I have never had to think about breathing, and yet here I was struggling to get air, feeling like it was being sucked from my lungs instead of filling them. When it came, it was in ragged little wisps that hurt, as if the air actually burned. I always figured that movies exaggerated the level of devastation, that the human spirit couldn't possibly be so fragile. It's weird, as I am no stranger to sorrow or struggle. I had always thought that I had paid my dues, worked hard on self-growth and acceptance in order to grow from my experiences rather then become stifled by them. I had truly believed that if you are good enough and work hard enough, eventually life will start to work in your favor and things will get easier. My motto before meeting Cam had been, "If only I can survive this, then it will be okay." And yet I had survived trials, pain, self-doubt, self-hatred, while having no idea how to survive or if I would, only to be asked to go through a pain so unimaginably horrific it stole all the joy of life I had worked so hard to find.

Day two: I lay on the couch unable to move, or at least unable to move my limbs in ways I want or feel I have control over. That doesn't mean they don't move themselves, though. My body has taken on a power of its own. One that I am slightly conscious of as I let the sobs rake through my entire body; shaking me with such strength I wonder for a second if I will fall from the couch onto the floor and then just as quickly dismiss the thought, because I really do not care anymore what happens. The unimaginable has happened, I am living my greatest fear, living the day I have spent dreading and trying not to think of and yet has haunted my mind and dreams for a year and a half. It has become a reality, my reality, the only reality I now know and am destined to face. So, I do not concern myself with worries about how cold I feel or that my shaking both from cold and the heart wrenching deep sobs might land me on the floor. I realize that my hands are moving all on their own, with no set purpose. I am simply withering on the couch. Withering in a pain so unimaginable that there are no words I can find to describe it. A pain that sucks the breath out and yet isn't compassionate enough to simply finish the job; rather still allows just enough air to keep me alive, to allow me to continue enduring its torture. My hands grab at my face, my neck, chest and arms. They scratch with no intention to scratch, in jerky unconscious movements. And my screams shatter the silence, startling me with their rawness. I have never heard something more real and uninhibited as the screams that left my throat that day, when my mom took my dogs for a walk and left me alone for a little bit. Somehow, I was able to find compassion for my dogs and didn't want to scare them more than they already were, so I waited until they were gone and then allowed my body to be taken over. Allowed the anguish to pulse through me, as I screamed louder and harder then I knew was possible. Screamed with anger, with sorrow, at the unjustness, at the lost dreams, the lost warmth. Screamed until my throat was so dry and ragged I was coughing and had to drink water to try to sooth it. And then, I lay there shaking with quiet tears rolling down my cheeks and wondered if I would ever be able to smile or laugh again. Wondered if anyone had ever felt a pain like mine, and if they did, how they ever managed to learn to live again.

Chapter Fourteen:
The Funeral

Anyone who has been called upon to plan a funeral knows that it is not simply a one day event. It is not simply a few hours, where a loved one is remembered or honored. No, it is far more than that. It takes hours of planning and preparation in order for it to run smoothly. And if others can leave at the end of the day thinking that the funeral was simply just those few hours, well then, it was done smoothly.

The planning of Cam's funeral started only hours after he had passed. I had barely had the opportunity to digest how he had actually left this earth, that I would never hug him again, never smell the pheromones I loved so much, and never complain about the smell of his breath. And yet I was required to begin thinking and planning the 'big event'.

Looking back, I understand that for many people the funeral can allow some closure, it makes it real for people, brings people together at a difficult time. And in hind sight it likely was a good thing we had it when we did, and it did force me to leave the house and not simply lay in a ball on the floor all day and night. But I still feel that it is somewhat unjust to require someone who simply wants to absorb what has happened and just cry about it, to have to make important decisions so soon. I knew Cam wanted to be cremated, that was something we had spoken about lots, as well as our plans regarding what would happen with his ashes. Cam always said that he would be dead and that it wouldn't matter what happened to his ashes; his only desire was that I did what I felt I needed to bring me peace. As it is hard to imagine what will bring you peace, we discussed a few options that I liked the idea of. We agreed that I would have his ashes made into jewelry by my mom's friend, so that I could always feel that he was with me, and that I would sprinkle his ashes on different hiking trails.

The morning he died, I spoke with my dad on the phone and told him the funeral would likely be in a couple weeks. I just didn't see the rush if he was being cremated. So you can only imagine my shock when I learned very shortly afterwards that a meeting with the funeral home was set for 2pm that very day! Cam hadn't been dead for 12 hours and yet I was supposed to go and talk to a complete stranger about how I wanted him to be remembered? It just seemed surreal to me. I repeatedly said to my mom that it simply was not fair, that no one should be required to think or do anything the first few days after losing the most important person in their life. I just wanted to check out of life, I just wanted a break. I was exhausted. I was exhausted from the last year and a half of struggling with the fear that one day I might lose him. I was exhausted from all that caretaking him in the last months had required. And I was exhausted from the massive amounts of adrenaline that had pumped through my body only hours before.

Above all, I was devastated and heartbroken while trying to come to grips that one journey was over, and that I was beginning another one, except this time Cam wouldn't be with me. But I obliged. I don't think I had the energy to argue or even request we wait a couple days. I just blindly got in the car and let my mom drive me to the funeral home, allowing the tears to stream down my face and sobs to rake through my body.

I remember finding it ironically funny that I was being asked to pick out the stationary for the guest book and service pamphlets. I wanted to yell, "Who fucking cares what design we have? I just lost my best friend, who I had planned on spending the rest of MY life with, why the hell would I care about the design on a piece of paper?" It just seemed so trivial; so unimportant in the grand scheme of things. In all honesty, the meeting was helpful and the person helping was good at slowly offering options and explaining everything in detail. I am grateful for that, but some of the things I was asked to decide on, or offer an opinion on, just didn't matter to me in the slightest. Then there were decisions that I wanted to be present for, wanted my brain to work for, but I just was so overcome with grief that I felt like I was a body that floated around and nodded but couldn't actually be present. I felt for the first three weeks like I had died at the same time Cam did; that I walked this earth and eventually even laughed and participated, but it was all in a dream like fashion and that, in reality, I had died that day with him. That feeling was very present those first two days. I ranged from numbed out to a bitter rawness of complete devastation.

Other than knowing he wanted to be cremated, I knew that I wanted there to be a video presentation of his life at the funeral. This was something that was important to me because I wanted people to be able to see the man I so deeply loved. Thankfully the funeral home was able to put this together for me, however it required that I go through all our photos and choose the ones that would best represent him and then put them in order along with what songs I wanted to play. In the end it was likely close to 15 hours of work since the photos were on various computers, phones, tablets, Facebook, etc.

I was concerned about how upsetting it would be to look at so many pictures of Cam; however, it brought me the only comfort I had those first few days. I realized that while I did not feel that he had lived long enough, and that I wanted so much longer with him, that he had lived a very good life while he was here, that we had done so much and that no one could ever take those experiences from me. Looking at our pictures over and over again helped me feel lucky rather than cheated; it helped me feel grateful rather than bitter; it reminded me that I was loved more deeply than many ever experience.

I am grateful Cam's parents were also at the funeral home and able to choose the cremation box as I was stuck in a dilemma of going with the cheapest option which has always been my automatic go to, and choosing something that was more expensive, but didn't resemble a plywood box you might burry a pet in. There were numerous points that day I thought, *"This is so useless. What is the point of any of this?"* How could I choose a box for my loved one to lay in, when all I wanted was for him to be in my arms? How could I choose stationary, when all I wanted was gone; when my dreams had been shattered and fears had all come true; when I was living my worst nightmare.

Then came the time to choose the urn that his ashes would go in. It's funny that Cam and I had talked about him being cremated, but I had never even contemplated an urn. Truthfully, I was shocked when they showed me the wall of all the urns to choose from, as I actually had pictured a Safeway bag filled with his ashes tied in a knot.

Yeah, I know that is completely unreasonable, but for some reason whenever I thought of having him cremated, I thought of a Safeway bag and had never questioned this image. Maybe it's because I always found urns slightly creepy and cold sitting on people's mantles. Yet here I was having to decide on the urn that would hold Cam's ashes, the urn that would somehow remind me of him. I remember standing there and not really seeing anything, just simply being so overwhelmed that I couldn't take in the images in front of me. It was my mom who pointed to a lovely little oval wooden box. It didn't look like an urn to me at all, but more like a large jewelry case or a keepsake box.

And then I saw the medallion on the top of it and knew why my mom had shown it to me. A lovely monarch butterfly was in flight with the words "In God's Presence" written. I was sold as soon as I saw the butterfly; Cam was the perfect butterfly who had been set free and transitioned into a beautiful angel.

Once all the details had been decided and the clothes for Cam to be cremated in were handed over, I was told that the obituary would need to be submitted by 1pm the following day. I am grateful writing comes fairly naturally to me, as I have no idea how the average person sits down to announce a nightmare in an elegant manner. It was imperative to me that his obituary honor who he was. I wanted people who did not know him to be left with a sense of what kind of person he was, and those of us who had lost him to be reminded of how lucky we were to have known him. Proclaiming his legacy was something I had control over and one of my last gifts to him. Once my mom drove me back to my house, I sat down at the computer and started writing. I just let it pour out of me. Who was Cam? What did he enjoy and love? What was his story? What was our story? His mom also wrote out an obituary which I combined into mine. Thankfully, they complemented each other, as she included elements I hadn't thought of about; where he was born and his younger years as well as all the family members' names who were left to miss him. The names of family, friends and his doctors mentioned in the obituary have been removed in order to protect their anonymity.

The family of Cameron announces his passing on Saturday, February 15, 2014 at the age of 28 years; shortly after spending a wonderful Valentine's Day with his wife Elizabeth. Cameron was born on May 11, 1985 at the Holy Cross Hospital, Calgary. He was always a curious and adventurous boy who became a kind and compassionate man. In 1992, Cameron moved to Brentwood where he made many friends. The "Brentwood Boys". He graduated from Sir Winston Churchill High School and Foothills Academy, where he first met Elizabeth.

Cam's booming voice, incredible sense of humor and ability to make people laugh, paired with his deeply philosophical side touched many people and will be forever remembered by all who loved him or simply were lucky enough to be in his presence. He was fiercely protective of his loved ones and would do anything to help those he cared for. He passed away after the bravest journey with spindle cell sarcoma. One in which he chose to see cancer as an opportunity for growth and change rather than despair. He was the living embodiment of the saying "live every day to the fullest." Throughout his journey, Cam remained hopeful, positive and often without meaning to, touched and changed people's outlook on life. He was extraordinarily stubborn and even as a small child would tell his parents, "You're not the boss of me." This stubbornness, while trying at times for those who loved him, proved instrumental in him refusing to simply give up to cancer. His wife, Elizabeth, stood bravely beside him and loved him deeply and dearly in every moment of their journey together. Together they strove to create a life-time of memories in a very short time. Their love was evident to everyone, but most importantly for Cam and Elizabeth there was never any questioning how they felt about each other.

Cam was a musician at heart who loved drum and base, as well as dub step. He took recording arts at school; however, he decided that this would be his passion and not his career. Early in 2014, Cameron became a journeyman electrician. Cam loved to go hiking with his wife, extended family and dogs Bentley and Mickey. It was on these hikes he truly became philosophical and came to terms with all that was going on in his life.

Cameron is survived by his wife, Elizabeth Leanne, whose love and devotion helped him through many difficult times both before and after his diagnosis with spindle cell sarcoma in 2012. (The names of those left behind have been removed to protect their anonymity.)

(A specific thank you to his Oncologists; names have been removed to protect their anonymity). Thanks to the compassionate and caring nurses at the Tom Baker Cancer Centre. And a very large thank you to all the Fire *and EMS personnel, as well as staff at the Black Diamond Hospital who treated Cameron and his family with such compassion at the most delicate of moments.*

And there you have it, a life summed up in a few words. However, in reality, there never could be enough words to describe or do Cam justice. I think that's partly where writing this book comes into play. I just want others to know Cam the way I did, to be impacted by his pure love for life the way I was and to understand what our journey was like. But the more I write, the more I realize I can only ever skim the surface.

Others could not possibly know him the way I did because you weren't there for all the hundreds of thousands of moments, and you could never understand the depth of our love or my sorrow at losing him. However, I do hope to allow you a glimpse and it helps me to realize our story wasn't just a lovely dream, it was my life, my miracle and how lucky I am to have experienced it.

When a person dies in the hospital and is picked up from the morgue by the funeral home, a relative has to come and identify the body before it can be cremated. In hindsight this makes perfect sense in order to avoid a mistake being made. However, learning the very day that Cam died and I had said my final goodbye to him, that I would have to return the next day to identify his body was almost too much to bear. I had had the strength to look at him one final time, to see him swollen, purple from lack of blood, cold and blood splattered skin. Had the strength to kiss him one final time, to stroke his face and clasp his hand to my cheek. And somehow I found the strength to put his hand down, to let go of it, to turn and look back once and then walk out of the room, the hospital and go back to our house, my house alone. Now I would have to do it all again.

I'm grateful that my mom and Cam's best friend came with me that day. Grateful that I did not have to walk into that room and see him in the cremation box that his parents had picked out, a lovely dark wooden box, on my own. He simply looked dead; it did not look like him, certainly not the man I fell in love with, who had made me happier than I'd thought was possible. No, that couldn't have been who was in the box, but yes, it was. I signed the piece of paper verifying that he, indeed, was Cameron, that I gave permission for this body of his to be burned the following day. Ashes to ashes, dust to dust.

Cam had made me promise after he died and came back to life in January that I would ensure that he really was dead before they cremated him. He was scared that they would make a mistake and that he would wake up in the fire. As much as I resented the fact that I had to identify his body, that this obligation fell to me as his wife, that so many difficult things had fallen to me over the last couple years, I was also grateful that I had been given the opportunity to come and see him. I leaned forward with tears streaming down my cheeks and flowing onto his face and kissed the top of his forehead.

It was ice cold, the night before he had been cold but this was like nothing I had pressed my lips against before. I nodded and said, "Ok, honey, I checked, you're really dead this time". It's amazing how you can have conflicting emotions all at once. I wanted to run and just keep running from that room and, at the same time, never wanted to leave. The funeral home had given me a red rose and I stood by Cam and kissed each of the pedals, telling them and him how much I loved him and would miss him, already missed him more than I ever imagined possible. I promised him again that I would be okay and that in time I'd be happy again, but had to go through this pain in my own way.

The thoughts that run through your head, when in such shock, can almost be humorous later on when looking back. One of the first things I had noticed when I approached the coffin was that his eyes were closed as if he were sleeping. This wouldn't have struck me as so odd had I not spent so much time the night before desperately trying to keep his eyes closed. I thought to myself that they must have glued them shut and almost reached out to see if I could open them, but remembered how they had looked the night before when I allowed them to fall open for a few moments and had looked into them. I remembered how it looked to see no life staring back at me and pulled my hand back not wanting to see what lay under his eyelids.

I also marveled at the make-up job that had been done, as he looked much better laying there than he had the night before. All the blood was washed away, and the purple had been evened out so that his skin looked a natural color. Had he not been so creepily still, I could have convinced myself he wasn't dead. I was grateful that they had taken the time to make him look presentable, and that he looked good in the clothes I had brought with me for him to wear, clothes we had picked out together only a year before. I laid the rose in his arms and stroked his cheek letting my hand rest on his crest, a chest I had never felt so still. Then I turned and walked out of the room and from the funeral home, full of such a deep sadness and bitter anger that this was my life, my story.

On February 19th, I sat with my family, at my aunt and uncle's house in Black Diamond, a five-minute drive from our home. My cousin left to go home, but called the house only minutes after leaving and very excitedly told her dad on the phone that there were Northern Lights outside. We all stumbled outside and, sure enough, there was a gorgeous display of Northern Lights all over the sky. For everyone else this is simply beautiful to look at, simply amazing as we rarely get them in southern Alberta. For me, I was angry so very angry at the unjustness of these beautiful Northern Lights showing up only 4 days after Cam died.

When Cam got diagnosed there were a few things that we discussed about what he wanted to do or see, the Northern Lights was one of them. We even went to the Yukon, which is where I grew up, in December one year to try and see them, but Cam never got the opportunity. And now here they were dancing across the sky, taunting me that Cam never got his wish, but I, who grew up seeing them, got to see them once again.

At home that same night I went to our bedroom window to close the blinds and was stopped dead in my tracks as the show outside was breath taking. The Northern Lights filled the sky and danced all around the hills and trees that our window overlooked. Suddenly, I realized this was far too ironic to be a coincidence, this was Cam giving me a sign that only I would know, that he was alright. I went to bed that night feeling blessed and even more loved, if that was possible.

I had been dreading the day of the funeral. I do not like to fall apart in front of people, especially people I do not know well. I did not know how I wasn't going to throw up, scream or just sob so loudly no one would be able to pay attention to what was happening. But none of that occurred. I was given more strength than I knew was possible to get through those hours. I woke up to the sound of birds singing outside my bedroom window. My first thought was 'today is going to be fine'. I had not heard birds singing yet that spring, and for some reason hearing them left me feeling like Cam was providing a perfectly, beautiful day. I stood at our bedroom window and simply smiled as all the hills were glowing a beautiful pink as the sun rose up into the sky. I knew I wouldn't have to do today on my own, that Cam would help me as much as he could.

Over the last few days I had been collecting items from around my house to bring to the funeral and set up a remembrance table, with things that meant a lot to Cam, had been a part of his life and would allow people who may have only known him in certain contexts to grow deeper in their understanding of who he was. It was also important to me that everyone who came and had known Cam, regardless of the age or stage of his life they had known him, could look at the table and see items that reflected the Cam they knew. It is amazing when you start to think about things that someone loved, (their hobbies, interests, work, accomplishments), how many items there are to choose from. It was easy to fill the 6 foot table and the floor encompassing the table also had larger items set up. I stood there looking at the table and surrounding area for a while before the funeral actually started, taking in each and every item, memorizing them all in my mind, tucking them away as little keepsakes of who Cam was.

Three of my closest friends, who had also gone to Junior High with Cam and me, had asked a few days before what we could do on the day of the funeral to all stand together and honor Cam in a way that would have made him laugh and appreciate. I had no idea, could not think of anything. Then one of them started laughing and said, "I know what Cam would find hilarious! We should go to the funeral with no underwear on." And so it was decided.

That was the first time I laughed since Cam died and while it felt weird and hollow, like a betrayal of him to laugh, it also felt good and right. Of course, as luck would have it I got my period the day before the funeral, a week early to boot. About ten minutes before we were to walk into the sanctuary where everyone was seated, I went to the washroom, put in a tampon, took off my underwear and stuffed them under the bag in the tampon and pad garbage container so that they would be hidden and walked out with a devious little smile on my face.

I knew Cam was getting a kick out of me walking around without underwear on at his funeral in a church, my personal own rebellion against all that was supposed to happen or how we are expected to behave. And I smiled again, after I learned that the girls had also gone to the washroom to stuff their underwear in their purses. We stood together and silently remembered and honored Cam in our own crazy way, that maybe only a young once very sexually active man could truly appreciate.

And then, it was time to walk into the sanctuary so the service could start. I focused on the ground in front of me and urged myself to walk forward. Every time the thought, 'this is MY husband's funeral, this is for Cam', startled me as if it were the first time I was having the realization, I burst into tears. Not the type I had feared where I would sob like I did at home. No, these were almost silent, just a stream of tears flowing from my eyes. I simply stared at the urn, which was surrounded by gorgeous flowers that I vaguely remember picking out only days before. How was it possible that a man with so much life and energy, a man that was so large in life, could be confined to such a small box? To the right of the urn was a beautifully framed black and white picture of Cam from our wedding day. I held his eyes and silently begged him to give me strength to carry me through this day.

In a weird way, I wish the service had been video recorded, as I was too emotional to fully take in all that was going on. However, I have had many people tell me it was one of the most amazing services they have ever been too and that Cameron was reflected perfectly. Even those who came to show respect, but had never had the pleasure of meeting Cam, stated that after listening to everyone speak about who Cam was and tell stories about him that they wished they could have met him. I find comfort in hearing this because it was important to me that everyone knew how amazing Cam was. That his interests be acknowledged and his absolute joy and love for life honored.

The exact words of the speeches have left me, the stories which were told have blended into the thousands of stories I know about Cam. But what has stayed with me is the messages in all of them. The message of love that Cam had, the message of being a curious and adventurous little boy, of being a loyal and hilarious friend. I remember being struck and feeling my heart warm even though it was hurting so badly, but I felt warmth creep in when hearing how very loved Cam was. A longtime family friend who had known Cam his entire life shared stories, which made us all laugh and cry, about Cam when he was just a little boy starting to find his way in the world. And then The Brentwood Boys somehow found the courage to support each other, as they always have, and all stood together as they each shared about their friendship and love for Cam.

The five boys who had grown up together had become four, and the pain at this loss was evident to everyone. Each of the boys stood up at the front wearing their beautiful hand painted silk butterfly ties they had all been given and wore to our wedding the previous summer. On that magical day they had worn black pants, a white shirt and their colorful ties, each of which matched their corresponding bridesmaid. Equally as handsome, but with heartbreaking differences, they wore black on black which meant that the ties stood out as a declaration of their unity as friends, no matter what happens. I specifically remember the feeling of absolute love, acknowledgement and appreciation each of the boys expressed to me in their speeches.

This has been echoed back to me by many of my friends; that they found it very moving how all the boys thanked me for loving their friend so deeply and taking care of him so well. Later that night, one of them, and I have no idea which one, thanked me again personally and stated that I had allowed all of them to continue simply being Cam's friends, to not have to change their roles and just be his buddies through everything because they all knew I was taking care of everything else. He thanked me for everything I did and for doing such a wonderful job. I hadn't realized until that moment that any of them had actually understood that had it not been for all I did, their lives and interactions with Cam would have been different. But they did get it and they had no problem letting me or the rest of the people know their gratitude, and for that I'll always be thankful.

They honored me as they honored Cam, and I know that there is nothing that they could have said or done that Cam would have appreciated more than to know they were taking care of me and would continue to do so.

I knew I wanted to speak. I had known that right away, but as it got closer to the day I began to question whether I would be able to read my speech and actually be understood through my tears. So it was decided that my mom would come up with me and possibly take over if I wasn't able to do it. But I practiced, just like I have practiced for everything I have the opportunity to do. I got to the point where I could read it without fully breaking down in tears and then I knew I was ready. I am a very driven person, but I also am very opinionated, and have some specific beliefs about how people should be remembered and whose duty it is to ensure that happens.

For me, I felt that I owed it to Cam to ensure people knew his wishes for them, that people celebrated his life and did not simply grieve his death. I know that I have zero control over how others choose to live their lives, but I do have control over the words I say and whether I choose to keep Cam's gifts to myself or share them with others. I chose the latter. Somehow, I found more strength then I knew possibly existed; however, I realized as I stood up there that I was not alone.

I had my mother on my left side, the Brentwood Boys all behind me, and many friends and family in front of me. Most importantly in that moment though, was how strongly I felt Cam on my right side. The entire time I read my speech I could feel Cam, could feel a sense of complete calm taking over and filling my being, could feel comfortable warmth radiating throughout my body. All of this together gave me strength to stand and give tribute to our love:

"Cam and I shared a love, bond and friendship most people only dream of. After his diagnosis, I used to remind him that this love was not limited to our bodies or this world, that no matter what happened, nothing could change our devotion to each other. I just never expected it to be so hard to be without his physical presence, even though I still feel him all around me, loving me just as he did in life. Many of you may have noticed on Wednesday night the Northern Lights that danced across the sky.

Something that is quite the rarity here in Southern Alberta. One of Cam's wishes was to see the Northern Lights before he died. This sadly was not meant to be. Being from the Yukon, they are very special to me and we had spoken of calling a daughter we might have Aurora for that very reason. I believe that Cam was sending us a message, one that he knew I would understand, that he is ok. Happy in the spirit world, but still with us. It simply is too perfect to be a coincidence. The Inuit say that the Northern Lights are our ancestors dancing in the sky for us. Cam continues to move us and bring awe, even after leaving this earth.

What many people may not know is that although loving each other always came very easily to Cam and me, it took work, compromise and change on both our parts to be able to function healthily in our relationship. Had it not been for the deep love we shared, I know neither of us would have been willing to do the amount of work that was required. I always told Cam "love is not enough, lack of love is not our problem; it's daily life". I feel honored, blessed and so, so lucky to have found someone who was willing to do whatever it took to make it work. I remember the day he quit drinking like it was yesterday, even though on April 17th it would have been four years. He sat there vulnerable and crying. He told me how much he loved me and that he wanted to spend the rest of his life with me, asked me what it would take to get me back. He agreed to stop drinking and work on communication, get couple's counselling, do whatever it took to make this the strong relationship it became. And he followed through on everything, just as he said he would, because that's who Cam was. If he knew something was important to someone he loved or if it was important to him, then there was nothing that would stop him from doing it.

Upon hearing his diagnosis, both of us felt paralyzed. Suddenly the future no longer held promise, but fear and uncertainty. But once again our love pulled us from that place and forced us to fully live in and embrace the present. To dive head first into life and soak it up. To create as many amazing memories as possible whether it was on trips outside of Calgary, hiking, yoga, dog walks or towards the end simply within our home, that we loved so much. Every moment came to count, is etched in my mind, because I feared one day I would be standing here and those memories would be all I had left. Cam fought hard to live, he embraced life, he was willing and grateful for all the crazy tinctures, pills, vitamins, juices and other things I researched and instructed him to take. It's hard to feel this now, but Cam and I often spoke about what a blessing cancer had been to his outlook on life and our relationship. Things were put into perspective and took on a clarity I believe they only can when you suddenly realize time is no longer on your side. Every moment counted and there were plenty where we would catch ourselves and say it wasn't worth the fight, wasn't worth being right. He adored me and loved me in ways I never realized a person could be loved or that I was worthy of. He taught me to love myself and managed to instill a confidence within me I have promised him, while he was still alive and worried about how losing him would affect me, will not be broken by my sorrow. I believe there are few people who could spend 122 days together between October 8th and February 14th, without seriously feeling cabin fever. And while we definitely had our moments, for the most part you would have been hard pressed to not see us in the same room or talking at any point during all those days. We were inseparable, completely in love, the best of friends who only grew to find the other more amazing, the more time we spent together.

Cam told me time and time again that I was his reason for living, that he didn't fear death; that he only feared leaving those he loved behind and how we would all cope. So once again, I stand beside his wishes, am his advocate and ask that we all remember how amazing he was, that we allow ourselves to grieve our loss, but we take care of ourselves and each other. That we don't give up on life or lose our spark, that this doesn't make us bitter. That we laugh hard, seek out fun and enjoy every bite of food we take. That we love and allow others to love us. These were Cam's wishes for us. It hurt him far more than anyone may ever realize to know he was powerless to save us from this pain. And so we owe it to him to live, and to live well. I always told him that every tear and all this heartbreak is worth it because I got all the laughs, joy and love. I would never trade those moments and memories for anything, even if it meant I wouldn't have to feel the sorrow I now feel. We came together as best friends at 14 and 15, we grew as a couple and eventually became one. I feel him with me still. The last thing he said to me was he didn't want to die without saying goodbye to me. When I asked him what he would say he told me how much he loved me, all he wanted for my life, all his dreams for me, and how grateful he was to have had me by his side every step of this journey. I didn't realize it truly was his goodbye, but treasure those words and those last minutes. Treasure that we were at home in our bed, in each other's arms with no knowledge or fear of what the next few hours, days and weeks would hold. There are no words to describe Cam, he simply was amazing, my best friend, love for life, inukshuk and the perfect butterfly. To have known him was to be blessed."

Those of us that had spoken all returned to our seats. I allowed myself to just let go and cry uncontrollably during the slideshow. I clung to my dad's hand with one hand and wiped my eyes with a continuous stream of Kleenex, which I simply allowed to fall to the floor around my feet. I consciously figured that today I was allowed to not worry about cleaning up after myself.

Every picture in the slideshow I had put in the order they were in. The songs I had chosen exactly how long they each would play for and what pictures they would correspond to. And yet, I had not seen how it all looked together. I could not have possibly expected it to have gone together better, to have depicted how adorable and sweet he was as a child, wild and crazy as a teenager, and amazingly goofy, dedicated and loving as a partner. The final song on the slideshow was by Jason Mraz "I won't give up", our wedding song; I had walked down the aisle to it in our first wedding, and it was our first dance at our second wedding.

It summed up our entire relationship, as neither of us ever gave up. You would have been hard pressed to find a dry eye in the entire church throughout the slideshow, and while my heart literally felt like it had been put in a food processer, I once again was moved by how full and amazing his life had been.

Ironically, similar to a wedding, at funerals there are receiving lines where the different family members stand in various corners of the room and people line up to give their condolences. I remember marveling at the sheer number of people who attended, which was over 400, and wanted to come and say a few words to me.

I had made it through the service. Somehow, I had survived and yet, here I was, required to continue holding it together a little bit longer. So I did the only thing I could and numbed out. I temporarily turned off and left my body. It was an absolute blur of people who came up to give hugs or offer a few words. Every face blended into the one before it and I would nod and exchange words with no idea of who I was talking to or what we were discussing. If I hadn't been exhausted already, this sucked all the energy I had left out. I vaguely remember one of my little sisters standing beside me with a plate of cheese and grapes on it that I picked at unconsciously.

I remember being surprised by people who came, that I had not seen in years, Junior High and High School teachers who had known Cam and I when we were simply best friends, and who I had not seen since I graduated. However, what stood out for me were the people who were not there or at least did not come up to me. The people who did not write or call, that did not explain why they couldn't make it. It was them who I remembered for the first couple weeks following the service. But like so much, I realized that everyone has their own story and that unless I asked each of them, I would not know why they were absent. So, while I did not fully compute those that were there, I did know that they were present, did appreciate them taking the time to come and to show support to me and respect Cam. In the moment, I may not have been able to put names to faces, but afterwards when I came back to my body, I remembered and I was grateful. Thank you to those who came, your love and support was felt even if I didn't realize it at the time.

Chapter Fifteen:
Single Again?

We live in a world where it is not all that uncommon to fall in love, think you found the perfect person, only to find down the road, you are again back on the market: SINGLE. Yet I never thought I'd be that person. When I reconnected with Cam, when he got sober and we worked so very hard to learn to appreciate each other's strengths and tolerate or even complement each other's weaknesses, I was sure I had found 'the one'.

And I had. He was everything I could have ever wanted and more. He loved and adored me in a way I had no idea I was even worthy of, let alone expected to find. I thought I was the luckiest woman alive, and indeed for a short time I was. He was my everything and I was his world. When you work as hard as we did to make something that you know has the potential to be beautiful, but has a few kinks in it, and then it starts to work all on its own with minor tune-ups along the way, suddenly life is no longer a struggle; it is simply beautiful.

After going through all that work, I realized I really had found the person that I could not only see myself spending the rest of my life with, but eagerly looking forward to spending the next 50 years with. I couldn't wait for all the experiences, good and bad, that we would have together. Suddenly, for the first time in my life, the future no longer held dread, because I knew that with Cam by my side there was nothing that I couldn't handle. I knew, or at least believed, that I would never be alone again. There is no greater feeling than to know the person you entrust with all your safety and happiness does the same with you and treasures every breath you take. And yet here I sit single.

That word feels like poison in my mouth. How can I possibly be a widow before I'm 30? How could I have only just started the fairy tale love story, to have it stripped away before I really even got comfortable? Single. Widowed. Alone. These words swarm around my head making me want to scream, beg for it not to be true, for it to simply be a horrible dream. I feel the vomit in my stomach start to threaten to overspill as I think about what I would put on a Plenty of Fish profile.

How can I think of dating when I already found my soul mate? I feel like I have used up my luck, that finding Cam and falling so deeply in love with each other is something many people never get to experience. So how can I ever hope to find something even slightly similar with another person? How dare I even hope for such luck? Yet at 29 my life looks long, and horribly lonely to think that I will never be loved again, never held or kissed. How can I possibly go on, without feeling desired and loved? And yet how can I accept those things from someone, when the one person I always wanted them from and gave them willingly to has been taken from me?

I stand trying to catch my breath in the shower. Trying to keep the vomit down as sobs take over my body. I feel lost between longing for Cam in a way I have never longed for another human and deeply desiring to be held and loved. I never was much for dating, never one for small get to know each other chit-chat. I've tried dating websites, and I've met some nice people, but it just seemed so set up and fake. The easiest part of being with Cam was how fast we fell in love and spending time together. We were best friends, we had history and there was no need to ever worry about what the other thought. It never crossed my mind that you wouldn't fart or go to the washroom in front of your partner right away. I know I didn't do these things with others I dated, but with Cam I felt more comfortable in my skin then I ever had, even on our first night together.

He made me feel beautiful, even when having a bowel movement. Within a week of dating he had coined the term 'poo hug', in which if one of us was going to the washroom, the other would sit on their legs facing them and we would hug and just talk. The level in which we were comfortable with each other is impossible to explain because there was nothing the other could do to gross us out or make us feel uncomfortable. We just wanted to be with each other every second. How can I possibly even expect to find someone who even remotely accepts me in the way that Cam did? How could anyone love me as deeply and completely? My friends have often thought our level of intimacy and comfort was a tad strange, and yet I have struggled to wrap my head around the concept that you could plan to spend your life with someone who wasn't willing to hold you while you smelt up the entire bathroom, or that you wouldn't be willing to make the same uncomfortable journey with them.

I realize with utter sadness that our acceptance and understanding of each other was a rare thing. I will likely never find someone who will be so comfortable with me and I them. How do I go from perfection to something else? How do I, who hates changing something that works, learn to be okay with something or someone different? I do not have these answers and they drive me crazy.

Cam did not want me to be alone. He hated the thought of me being with another person, but he made it clear to me that he didn't want me to be single forever. He even joked that I had to start dating in the first six months of him dying, because otherwise I'd get old and set in sadness. I have promised I'll try when I feel ready to date. I'll open my heart and mind to meet someone new. Yet that seems a daunting task, and one that is sure to fail. I feel destined to be alone forever, or stuck in a relationship which is good and satisfying, but not enriching. I'm single and available. I'm young and beautiful. I'm the full package as Cam always told me, "brilliantly smart, hilarious, goofy, confident, compassionate, understanding and the most beautiful woman in the world." And

I'm now alone. And the only person I want, the only person I've ever wanted, is the only person I can't have.

So I sit and twirl the two rings on my left ring finger. Rings that held so much meaning when Cam placed them on my finger. Rings that held so much promise, so much happiness and love. One day I will have to take them off, I know this. I know that they no longer hold any significance, as the person these rings signify I am married to, no longer walks this earth. They simply are a reminder of what was and what no longer is. They feel like a lie, like I am walking around pretending to belong to a group that I have unwillingly been cast out of. Wearing them feels like a joke, and yet I cannot bear to take them off. I desperately do not want to accept that this is my fate, my reality, there is no hiding from the truth that I am alone and single. Once the rings have been removed, I am announcing this to the world. My finger will be barren. The place where rings we had chosen together, and were supposed to sit until the day I died will be empty; perhaps never to be filled again.

Chapter Sixteen:
I Want You Back

I want you back. How often have I silently sobbed each of those words? Lying on my bed alone, unable to move, as the pain, which radiated from my heart throughout my body paralyzed me. "I want you back". Plain and simple. There is nothing else that needs to be said, no other phrase that can explain what I feel more completely. That is my wish, my longing. All I long for every single day; all day and all night. I repeat it over and over, until it leaves a bitter taste of agony on my tongue because I know the one thing I ask for is the one thing I cannot have. He is not coming back. Not now, not ever. This is different than a break up, there is no pretending it is only temporary, and daydreaming about a different happy ending only leaves me more heartbroken. No, this is my reality, the only one that will ever be, as I cannot go back in time and in a moment everything changed forever. My sobs gain momentum until I'm yelling, begging and pleading for him to come back; to not leave me all alone. I give into the screams, not caring if my neighbors hear me. And eventually my voice breaks, and I lay there coughing, choking on tears that I wish would drown me, as going on living is far less appealing than joining Cam wherever he is. But they don't drown me. I lay frozen, shocked and uncertain about this reality I have found myself in, and say the only things I know to be true anymore, "I love you so much", "I miss you more than I knew was possible" and "I want you back, would do anything to have you back."

And, of course, he doesn't come back. Somehow, I manage to get dressed and go out in public. Somehow, I manage to smile, laugh and joke with people, to look so happy, to talk about how good I'm doing, all while knowing my pillow's still wet from last night's tears and the fresh ones that fell when I woke to an empty bed and realized all over again that Cam is gone. "I want you back" are the first words I utter after turning off my alarm and staring at his side of the bed, feeling the indent in the mattress where he lay so many nights just inches from me. "I want you back", the last words I silently repeat like a mantra every night as I wait for the sweet release of sleep. One wish, one longing.

Chapter Seventeen:
Visits from Heaven

I always told Cam that our love was stronger than death, that nothing would keep us apart. Cam began making his presence known to me from the first day he died. At times it is possible to dismiss it, or almost not pay attention to it; other times there is no denying what I have felt or heard. I have chosen to not dismiss any sign that brings comfort. I have decided that it is not my job to determine what is coincidence versus Cam sending messages, thus I embrace them and allow myself to be comforted. Whether it's by a friend calling or texting right when I was feeling overwhelmingly alone, or a song coming on the radio with words that I do not even need to use my imagination to see Cam saying to me. There are messages all around me, as long as I'm willing to receive them, smile, cry and thank him.

My cousin and I went to the drumming circle that Cam and I used to try to go every Friday night for a few months after he was diagnosed. We both loved it. Cam being a drummer would have his hands on the drum from the moment he walked in till the time we got into the car to leave. He really was at home and at peace there. My only regret is that we stopped going and let our busy lives and new interests take the place of this one. There is about one to two minutes during the drum circle where the lights are turned down very low and everyone drums as hard as they can and screams at the top of their lungs.

This was the reason I kept going back, this was my outlet, my saving grace as I felt my world fall apart around me. There are not many places in the world you can go and just scream without worry of someone hearing you and thinking you're in need of help. I would scream so loud and hard that my throat would be ragged for the rest of the night and sometimes into the next day; scream so hard that my whole body would shake and eventually my screams would turn to sobs which travelled through my body. I never felt judged there. We all felt pain and we all were there for different reasons, but it helped ease the pain. I was able to let out my anger at having the love of my life get cancer when we were just starting out our life. I was able to expel some of the absolute devastation and fear I felt about my future. This allowed me to stay present with Cam the rest of the week, and it allowed me to not dwell in the possibilities of tomorrow rather just what was going on today.

And although Cam never claimed to look forward to the screaming round as much as I did, he sure would let it out every week, and I saw his quickness to respond in anger or become agitated begin to decrease substantially. He began to talk about cancer as being an eye-opening experience and not of it being something to be feared or hated. These drumming circles were instrumental in allowing us a safe place to get mad at the injustice we had been handed, and to let it all go and then make beautiful music while having pure and simple fun. After his death, I was able to scream and cry about the absolute devastation I felt, the rawness of all my emotions and how unjust I still feel it is, even if I trust there was a reason for it. I was able to just let go and really lose it for a couple of minutes until the ache in my heart wasn't quite as big.

I felt Cam so very strongly in the drum circle; I felt his energy just dancing around the room as we beat our drums from around the world. When my hands touch the top of his drum, I feel like I'm connected to him. I wasn't allowed to use his drum when he was alive, because he just couldn't bear to not play it, even for a few minutes; he just loved it so much. Luckily, lots of drums were provided and I always used one of those. I feel like I can feel his hands on the drum's skin, like I am soaking him in through my palms every time I hit the top of our drum. He is there, I know it without a doubt.

The night I went with my cousin the facilitator asked us to do something different that I had never experienced at a drum circle before. She asked us to close our eyes and she dimmed the lights. She then asked us to all think of a loved one who has passed on and to send loving energy to them. She spoke briefly about this, although I was already drifting inside my own mind and away from the group. It was then that Cam came to me in a vision, or I guess Cam and myself came to me.

We were standing in a beautiful field of flowers, with snow covered mountain tops in the distance. I watched the scene as if it was a movie, while being acutely aware of being right there at the exact same time. It was the first time I have seen myself, as a part of a vision. It was vastly different from a memory or daydream. Cam kissed me over and over while holding me. I held his face between my hands as we kissed and then wrapped my arms around him and just clung to him. We went between kissing, touching each other's faces, holding each other so tight I could actually feel the pull on my back and entwining our fingers together, and just looking at each other while talking. Each of these I felt in my body as if it were happening, as I watched it unfold in my mind.

Tears streamed down my face as I sat quietly in the drumming circle. I told Cam how much I missed him and how little I wanted to go on in this world without him. I repeated over and over how much I loved him. All of his words have not stayed with me; however, they were not the exact words I was meant to remember, but rather the message he gave me. I was reminded of how very deeply he loves me, that he still loves me and that he will always be with me, that nothing can ever happen that will take him away from me. I had a very peaceful realization that this vision was a glimpse of our spirits connecting in just as real a fashion as we did physically, when he walked this earth with me; that although I crave his body and miss his touch in this dimension not all of me is without him.

When I realized it was getting time to return to my body and leave this beautiful meadow with him, I cried harder and told him I didn't want to go, I didn't want to leave him. And this I remember as I tucked it away for safe keeping; Cam held my face and told me that I can return to that meadow to talk to him whenever I need to, that he will always be with me and meet me there if I need anything. Then he took my hands and kissed me. And in no uncertain terms he reminded me that I still have a mission to carry out on earth, that I have not fulfilled my purpose yet and that he will help me, but I need to continue on. I realized as I was coming back to my body and let go of his hand that what I saw, where my spirit had gone was not only where I could go anytime I need to connect with him and talk freely; it is where I will go once my journey is done on this earth. I was given a rare gift, that many never have, the gift to see where their spirit will one day go once they have completed their purpose.

I know I cannot rush that day and that I must live the remainder of my life, however long that may be, to its absolute fullest for both Cam and myself. Yet, I would be lying if I didn't say that I do look forward to joining him permanently in our place, our meadow; but until then I'll just visit from time to time and keep my eyes, ears and heart open for all the signs he gives me every day that he loves me and is even closer to me in death then he ever could have been in life.

Chapter Eighteen:
A Picture Says 1000 Words

Our memory is a funny thing. It chooses to hold onto certain images, it can haunt us with flash backs of images that we long to forget, wish we never experienced. Or it can let those fade away. For the first few weeks after Cam died, all I could picture was him lying in the coffin. The image of how he looked the night he died was etched into my brain. Every time I closed my eyes, I saw him still, unmoving, dead. Yet slowly it passed, and I started to remember him as I had known him the majority of our time together.

I began to remember how he looked during his last summer we were together, remembered how he looked when he was the most fit and healthy he had been in his entire life. I realized that the way he had looked the last few months of his life was not how I would remember him in the long run, as those few months were such a short period in the totality of our relationship. I have so many more memories of the healthy Cam than I do of the dying or already dead one. So, why would those memories be the ones I choose to hold onto? Initially, when working on the slideshow for his funeral, I was shocked at the pictures and struggled to even remember him when he was in such great shape, as the drug dexamethasone, had bloated him and changed his appearance substantially.

Now when I look at pictures from his last Christmas or Valentine's Day, the night that he died, I am amazed as that is not how he now looks in my memory. Time is a funny thing, but I am happy the images of him in the hospital bed turning a deep purple have left my mind unless I call on them, and the image of him lying in a coffin in a shirt I had picked out with him only a year before, has also lost some of its clarity in my mind. That was not Cam, it was not how he would want me to remember him. And thankfully it isn't how I remember him now, but that took a few weeks to accomplish.

Chapter Nineteen:
Doing It All On My Own

This isn't what I wanted. It's not what I signed up for. I wanted a partner who I could share the responsibilities with, share the load. I did not want to be on my own trying to run a house and yard by myself. If I had wanted this, I would have bought a house in Victoria and not a condo. And when Cam wanted the big house with the big yard so we could grow into it and raise a family together, I let him know that all yard work and any repairs would strictly be his responsibility. I wanted no part of any of it. Now that may sound unfair and unrealistic, but that's how I felt and I wanted him to know where I stood before we made a huge purchase. And while he was able, Cam upheld his end of the deal. He loved being outside and in the garden, mowing the lawn, pulling weeds, connecting to the earth. That was his meditation space and he took pride in how it looked. I just enjoyed it from a distance. I never realized or fully appreciated all the things Cam did without me even knowing. The spiders he would carry outside, the hot water tank he would relight without needing to be asked, the grass he cut and weeds he pulled.

But Cam is gone. And now it's just me. I'm on my own, and all the things I explained right from the start I wanted nothing to do with, are now my sole responsibility. I suddenly, and very unwillingly, became a one woman show. This was never what I wanted. I am angry. I did not want to have an overrun garden, did not want huge weeds everywhere and surely did not want grass that is so long that you can't walk around the yard. I sat down in our almost knee-high grass one morning the first summer I was on my own and started to cry because I just didn't know how to do it. My uncle had come over and shown me how to start the lawn mower the first time, but time had got away on me and I hadn't been out in a while. Starting it was fine but keeping it going was a whole other story. I couldn't walk for more than two feet without it stalling. I now realize that the grass was simply too long and wet for the mower to handle, but at that time I thought there was simply something I was doing wrong; a trick everyone else knew but I did not. I longed for Cam as I sat defeated in the grass; yearned to hear him laugh and tell me to move aside so he could fix the problem. I felt paralyzed with fear and dread for my future, one I was facing on my own. If I can't mow my own lawn, how can I possibly run a whole household and be okay? I sat and cried in my long, wet grass for everything I had lost, for the fact that I was so utterly alone and for my fear of my future.

Regardless of how alone, scared and angry as fucking hell I may be, the reality is that this entire house and all the surrounding jungle property is my responsibility now. I inherited it. And somehow, I have to figure out how to take care of it. The panic that I can't do it, that I will fail, that I have no idea what I'm doing, that it is simply too much work for me to do on my own, rises every single time anything has to be done, anything goes wrong or any decision needs to be made. I was almost ready to sell the house the day I realized the pilot light had gone out on the hot water tank and sat there with my head in my hands sobbing, "I need you, where are you? Why did you have to go away and leave me alone?"

I managed to remember to just read the directions (about 8 times before attempting). And although I thought I was going to throw up due to being so scared I would do it wrong, it started and I had done it. In that moment, I thought I had conquered the world. It may seem so trivial, like such a small thing to cry over or to be beyond proud of yourself for, but if you have ever found yourself alone and fully responsible when you so desperately don't want to be, then you understand. And if you haven't, well, I pray you never do.

Chapter Twenty:
A New Identity

So if I'm not a wife, and technically I no longer am, then who am I? I'm no longer a caretaker. No longer a lover. No longer anyone's main person, their constant, their rock, their everything. I'm just me. But who is that? When did I lose myself in this relationship? How did a strong opinionated feminist, like myself, lose all sense of who I am?

I remember the sharp shock that rocked my very core the first time someone introduced me as "the widow". I felt exposed, vulnerable, betrayed, as if that was all I was now. I had been Cam's wife and now I simply was a widow. There was or is no room in that identity for all the other parts of me who make me who I am. But at that time, in those very early days of learning to walk on my own without him here on earth, I truly did not feel I had an identity outside of him. But a widow? Before I was 30? It was too cruel to be true. That word was for the elderly, who had seen their silver wedding anniversary, had watched their children grow old, and held their grandchildren. It was not a word I wanted to embrace or accept as a part of my identity. My feeling toward this word, while never one anyone wants to have applied to them, has shifted time and time again over the months since Cam died. Some days I use it, as it's a simple well understood word in our society.

It is the ticky box that I must check when asked if 'single,' 'married', 'divorced' or 'widowed'. But I am coming to see all the parts of me that that word can never express. I am finding me again. I am discovering parts of myself I had forgotten about while in the relationship, and some are still no longer a use to me, but others I have begun to fan like a coal from an old fire slowly bringing those aspects back to life. I have begun to look at aspects of myself that developed while in a relationship with Cam and similarly evaluated which parts I want to keep and which no longer serve me now that he is gone.

I specifically treasure the many, many gifts he blessed me with, particularly how he helped me understand that I am worthy of love and how, as a result, I have opened my heart to allowing, accepting and even expecting others to love me. Those aspects of myself I refuse to let go of because they were his greatest blessings to me and he worked so hard to get me to a place where I truly felt love for myself. And possibly most exciting and terrifying at the very same time, has been discovering who I am now that he is gone, now that it is just me.

Terrifying, because what if there isn't anything all that great? What if people only hang out with me out of pity or obligation to Cam? Alarming, because it has been so long since I only thought of what I wanted to do, or what I liked with no real need to consider how my actions might impact another person. There is a kind of freedom in suddenly finding yourself on your own again, with just you to worry about. Not the kind of freedom anyone wants, certainly not the kind of freedom I ever wanted, and most definitely a kind of freedom that I would give up in a second to have Cam back. But nevertheless, it is a kind of freedom. And freedom can be terrifying. There is lack of structure, lack of expectations, lack of a road map to follow. While it was a freedom I did not want, I realized that it was one I could deny and hide my head in the sand or I could start accepting and decide what I would do with this freedom.

This led to the inklings of excitement, which would come up in little unexpected bursts. It was as if every once in a while I was meeting myself for the first time. Almost like I was someone that I had heard so much about that I felt like I knew them, but now I was actually getting to meet them for the first time and really sit down with them and ask 'what makes you tick?', why, when everything fell apart and you so desperately did not want to be alive, did you make the decision not to join Cam?', 'what brings you joy?', 'what do you want to accomplish?', 'what are your dreams for *your* life?', 'what really sustains you when everything else falls away?'. Some of these answers came easily to me, some surprised me and some continue to change as I continue to grow and re-meet myself.

I remembered how much I loved biking when I lived in the Yukon while growing up, as well as when I would visit my family there in my early 20s. One of the things I loved most about living in Victoria, while doing my Bachelors and Masters of Social Work, was that my bike was able to be my main mode of transportation. It was on my bike rides to and from the University of Victoria that I would dream of one day owning a road bike, as I had been using the same mountain bike since I was 12 years old and it was heavy and not kind to me on hills. But this dream had always been put on hold, as I couldn't justify the money, when in reality my mountain bike still worked for the maximum two hour rides I did. It was not until I clipped into the peddles of my new road bike, as I set off on my first training ride for the Ride To Conquer Cancer a 228km bike ride over two days through Kananaskis Country, that I remembered just how much I loved biking and my desire to own a road bike.

Waves of emotion washed over me, as I road from our beautiful home in Black Diamond to Okotoks. Gratitude that he had convinced me to move to such a beautiful remote part of the province, amazement that I had forgotten how free I felt when on a bike, excitement that I was going to be training for something that was far more physically demanding than anything I had attempted to do in the past, and deep sadness that I was doing it all without Cam to share it with. Yet there was something else; there was a rising sense of peace, a sense of connection to myself, to the universe, and to Cam. This connection felt deeper than can possibly be expressed, it transcended time. It filled my core.

For three months I trained on the various country roads around our home: I sang songs out loud to the cows, stopped and ate protein bars while chatting to the horses, screamed deep anger at the top of my exhausted lungs at the mountains, sobbed for all I had experienced, lost, and feared. I spoke constantly to Cam while riding. It became my time to reflect and connect with him. I came to view those rides as a date with myself and with him, saw my relationship with Cam transcend, from one of longing for what once was, to one where I appreciated what we currently had and the ways he showed me he was still very much a part of my life. I pushed through the physical pain of a sore bruised bum, chaffed inner thighs and private parts, cramping legs, and extreme thirst, because I knew that this physical pain was nothing compared to what I had witnessed Cam go through, or anywhere close to the emotional anguish I was slowly learning to heal from. I found my legs again on my bike.

I once again began to see and truly appreciate nature's beauty. I came back to life. I learnt a lot about my character on those rides. I realized that I wasn't going to give up on myself, just like I hadn't given up on Cam. I found parts of myself I had forgotten, or never knew existed on those old country roads. I realized and was able to acknowledge and give myself credit for, just what kind of person I truly was. I came to realize I had survived the unimaginable and that not only had I survived, but I was growing in spite of it, that I was willing to do something I never would have thought possible before Cam died.

I realized that life had been put in perspective. I realized that I had faced my greatest fear, I had lost the love of my life, my best friend, my husband, that I was now all alone. I had faced this fear, I had lived it, was living it and it didn't kill me. It almost did, but I loved life enough to keep fighting. I remembered the beauty of life and trusted that one day I would truly smile again. I had undergone a challenge far greater than I could have anticipated, far more exhausting and challenging than anyone may ever realize, and I did it. With those realizations suddenly I was 'dangerous', because I knew there was nothing I couldn't do, there was nothing that could stand in my way, there was nothing I couldn't survive. And physical pain over a few hours or even days had nothing on what I had lived through. I set out to do the Ride for Cam, and he remained who I rode for; but in the end, I also did it for myself.

The Calgary Herald caught wind of Cam and my story, as well as that I was planning to do the Ride to Conquer Cancer and two days before the Ride featured our story (See Appendix Four). The ride ended up being amazingly moving and therapeutic in itself. I felt strong and ready, I enjoyed nearly every second of it, and I was so proud of myself. Other bike riders or supporters on the side of the road, who saw my name and recognized it from the Calgary Herald, called out to me. Many of them I rode with for a short period of time, sharing our stories, listening to how touched and motivated they were by mine. Once again, I was reminded that people care, that people want to make a difference; they sometimes just don't know what to do. I was reminded that I wasn't alone, and that together we can and are writing a different story for future families who find themselves sitting in a hospital room hearing the dreaded words leave the doctor's mouth and wondering how this can now be their life.

Cam's funeral

His urn at the funeral

**The table with various items
which meant something to Cam at his funeral.**

Picture gifted to Elizabeth shortly after Cams funeral
of the Northern Lights on February 19, 2014.
His 'message' to Elizabeth that he was okay.

Elizabeth training for the Ride to Conquer Cancer

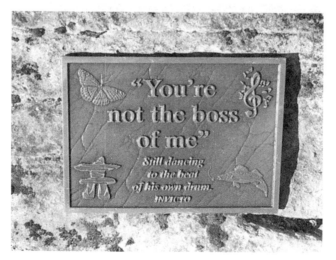

The plaque where Cams ashes were scattered

The family of trees protecting the rock
with Cams plaque and his final resting place.

**Elizabeth scattering Cams ashes
with one of his best friends on June 29, 2014**

**Cam and Elizabeth's wedding rings
and her engagement ring combined together.**

Chapter Twenty-One:
Letting Go Of Our Baby

How do I decide whether or not to have Cam's child? I still have rights to his sperm that are frozen in the fertility clinic, simply waiting for me to show up with the money and a healthy uterus. I feel so much guilt at the thought of not using the sperm to have his child. It just seems like such a waste to not use it. All the time, effort and money we put into saving it and keeping it protected. It feels like I am throwing the last part of Cam away. I have so many dreams tied up in having his child, holding his baby, and the feeling that he could somehow live on in his child; almost like I hadn't lost him. It was always our plan that I'd use the sperm, and yet now I don't know if that will manifest.

I do not want to be a single mother. It is not an easy task to sign up for. It is not what I want for me or my child. I marvel at the strength of all the single mothers out there, but that is not what I want my future to be if I can help it.

If I am 35 and still not with anyone, then I do believe that I will use his sperm, as it is more important to me to have the opportunity to be a mother, even if that means a single mother. Yet what if I meet someone? And I desperately hope I do. How do I ask someone else to be okay with me having Cam's child? How do I ask someone to raise a child that is not their blood, a child that I did not have when we met? How do I ask this of someone who is able to have their own child? Would they not feel that I value Cam's sperm more than their own? That it is more important to me to have his child than theirs? These questions run through my mind on a regular basis, they drive me crazy with fear that I will never have Cam's child or that I will lose someone I care about, when I broach the subject.

I don't want the person to take it to mean that I don't love them, want their children, or that they aren't good enough. I want both children, I want one of Cam's and one with my new partner, but how crazy a request is that? Having Cam's child is something I have thought about and planned for the last five years. We planned to do this together. It's hard to let go of this dream when it could be a reality. When his sperm is all that is left of him. When I have the ability to ensure that his genetic line does not stop with him. But that is a large responsibility and weighs heavy on my conscious. Realistically, I know that if I love my next partner I will not break up with them if they say that they cannot honor my desire to have Cam's child, honor my request to have them raise his and my child as their own. Yet, I am not ready to let the dream of having Cam's child go. (See Appendix Five for final decision).

Chapter Twenty-Two:
Salt In The Wound

When you normally think of death, and the grief of those left behind, you likely think of the sadness that goes along with the loss of the physical person, the loss of potential dreams that will now never be fulfilled, the loss of everything you loved about them that you will never have again. And each of these losses is tremendous. They each can and often do repeatedly knock you on your ass and leave you winded. But for those of us who have been the main caretaker, who are the executor of the estate or who, in cases like mine where there was no Will and yet were the closest relation, the responsibility naturally falls, we know all the various layers others do not have to acknowledge.

While others can curl into balls and reminisce, while sobbing, or get angry and ask all the 'why' questions, or even become incredibly busy and distract themselves from the pain of loss, we are forced on a daily basis, for so very much longer than anyone would ever expect, to manage the mess that is left. There were the phone calls, cancelling things, and transferring other things into my name. Each of those phone calls or meetings left me feeling like I was going to be sick; I saw each of them as a tie to Cam that I was cutting. It would take at least 30 minutes to convince myself to pick up the phone, that it was time, this had to be done, that there was no denying it.

Rationalizing to myself that not making the call wouldn't bring him back. Yet removing his name from our Telus account, switching Enmax into my name, cancelling Costco and bank accounts, arguing with cell phone companies that it did not seem fair to have to pay a cancellation fee, when he had passed away, as well as the dozens of other phone calls and meetings. Each felt like a slap in the face, saying that he was not coming back, that I was fully and completely alone now.

I did not want to make these calls, had never thought about them as a part of losing him; they seemed insignificant compared to the vast emptiness I knew I would feel when I couldn't curl into his arms and rest my head on his chest. But they haunted me, the knowledge that I had to make the calls left me feeling more anxious than I can possibly explain. Making them left me feeling vulnerable, exposed, alone and hopelessly devastated. Opening my mail and seeing only my name on the bills was a shock every time, and resulted in me putting off going to the post office for days at a time.

After hanging up the phone, the realization of what I had done was sickening. It was like being forced to relive over and over, that Cam was really and truly gone, he was dead, it was just me now; everything was my responsibility and mine alone. Someone could think that this might have had the potential to be an empowering experience, to see that I can do it all on my own.

Do not be fooled, there was no empowerment. I simply endured and tried to become a robot who did what was needed, mailed or faxed death certificates as was required, and answered all the questions asked surrounding when he died, how and what my plans now were. Not every call was horrible; some companies have obviously come up with policies that allow the transition to be fairly simple; not quick, but simple. I always sighed with relief when I made one of those calls, when all I had to do was explain that my husband had passed away and I wanted to switch the Visa card and name on the account.

However, not all companies are so generous. And it was these experiences that made this already very difficult time almost unbearable. I spent hours and hours over the months following Cam's death on the phone or in offices, providing copies of our marriage certificate and his death certificate trying to show that I had the right to make changes, that if they didn't give me the right, there would be no one else, as the only person they were willing to speak with was currently in an urn sitting on my living room floor.

My frustration at having to prove my worth, as Cam's spokesperson, and the inability to move forward with certain aspects of the estate, made me furious. I felt dread every time I had to make a phone call to those difficult companies, every time I knew I would be fighting to convince another of what I so desperately didn't want to believe; Cam is dead, gone, not coming back. I'm all that's left.

Chapter Twenty-Three:
Comparing Grief?

I have never been a competitive person. Indeed, I run away from anything with competition, as I hate to lose and hate watching others lose, so essentially I am in a lose-lose situation. Yet, grief brings out the worst in people; though at times it can bring out good aspects, eventually pain usually results in our ugly sides rearing their heads.

When Cam initially died, the pain I felt was so all encompassing, intense and devastatingly raw that I did not believe that anyone else had ever felt something like it, nor would anyone understand the level of my sorrow. I could not contemplate that people could survive such agony; assumed that this level of pain would surely destroy them. It was a pain so unexplainable, that I prayed no one would ever know its depths. While I understood Cam's family and friends were also all hurting, could see their pain and hear them speak of it, I did not think it possible that their pain could be of the same magnitude as my grief. My brain could not comprehend that others would be strong enough to continue living, if they too were suffering so much from losing Cam. I, myself, thought of death, numerous times a day, of ways to escape the appearance of everlasting agony. I could not imagine living without him, and my potentially long life stretched out in front of me as a jail sentence I was frantic to escape.

Yet, Cam had made me promise numerous times, from the time he was diagnosed, that I would not kill myself if he was to die. After he passed, I cried what felt like endless tears, and apologized to him that I could not keep that promise, that I hadn't realized how hard it would be, that he hadn't understood the level of absolute agony and loneness being the one left would entail. I did not understand, if others felt the same pain I did, how they were still alive, how were we not all dying? But I didn't kill myself; somehow, I found the strength to bargain with myself that I would make it through that day and could die the next, or that I needed to do certain things and then it would be okay to take my life.

Ultimately, it was the care of my dogs and caring about what would happen to them that kept me here. I watched them struggle to understand their changing world, and the uncertainty of the emotions within the home. They became aggressive with each other, trying to release the tension and fear by fighting. My heart broke for them, as they simply did not understand what was happening, where their dad went and why their mom could not stop crying. Somehow, in my intense moments of grief I found compassion for these two furry angels that Cam had begged me to get; these amazing gifts he gave me. I did not know who would take them, if they would be kept together, how many walks a day they would get, if their lives would be as pleasant as Cam and I had tried to make them.

So, I decided that I would stay alive for them; that I would endure a pain more devastating than I thought would be humanly possible, because I loved them more than I needed to escape that pain. Now, if I am fully honest, the idea of killing both of them before killing myself did cross my mind a few times after I decided I could not leave them alone. However, I also could not bring myself to hurt them, to end their lives before it was their time.

As time passed the desire to leave this earth and escape the pain began to lessen. I began to re-engage in life, to laugh again, to have true moments of joy and fun, to realize that somehow, as incomprehensible as it was, life continued without Cam; and that life could be enjoyable. I began to realize that just because none of us had killed ourselves to escape the pain of losing Cam did not mean that anyone's pain was greater or lesser than the next. That essentially it was impossible to compare our grief.

Cam had filled a different role in each of our lives, he had had a unique relationship with each of us, and no one else would ever replace that for any of us. He had been our Cam and the loss to each of us was as individual as our relationship had been with him. There was no comparing, and comparing did no good. This was not a competition I was interested in winning or engaging in. We hurt, we missed him, we did our best to survive, and that looked different for each of us.

I think one of the greatest mistakes people make is judging the way another grieves. I know I was guilty of it, would wonder about the different ways people were coping, but I also had the education and understanding that we all grieve and manage that grief differently. I watched as some withdrew from everyone or pushed loved ones away, some reached out and became overly social trying to distract themselves from the pain inside, some cried easily or seemingly nonstop, and some appeared as if nothing has changed, as if Cam never even existed or the loss has been meaningless. There are numerous other ways that I witnessed people cope with the loss of Cam. And I've come to realize that no response is a better indication of the level of pain than the next.

Since the time of Cam's death I have devoured book after book on loss. Books written by spouses outlining their personal stories of struggling with a loved one's illness and eventual death; books on how they coped after their partners had left this earth; books written on how to survive anniversaries or holidays; books on the stages of grief; books that almost provided a road map regarding how to maneuver this unchartered territory; books about grief of spouses, siblings, children, parents, etc. I was looking for the answer of exactly how to do this.

While I did not get that answer, as it is different for each person, I did get clarity that people all over the world are making this journey every day, and somehow the pain doesn't kill them, although it feels like it will at times. And thus it was logical to conclude that I, too, would likely make it through alive.

I still have an adverse reaction when I hear people make comments that compare the types of grief. Comments that may be meant to offer comfort or possible understanding, yet minimize and dismiss another's pain in the same instant. I have no idea what it is like to lose a parent, as both of mine are still alive, nor have I lost a sibling, child or any other family member. I have lost a few very close friends at ages where their lives were just really starting, and I have lost my best friend who became my husband, my everything. And there are similarities in my experiences of losing friends as others who speak of losing friends, just as there are similarities in my experience of losing Cam as others who I have spoken to who lost their husband. Yet they are not exact and even then cannot be compared. My relationship with Cam was different from theirs with their husband and thus how we grieve will also be different.

So I struggle when I hear people talk of loss of a child as being greater than any other loss. Is it an unimaginable pain? Absolutely. Is it the order we wish things to go? No, it is not. Is it every parent's worst nightmare? Most definitely. And I will not pretend to imagine how devastating it would be, as I was not blessed with children and thus cannot truly comprehend what it would be like to lose one. But I do intimately know the horrors of losing one's spouse, of realizing that the future you had tied up in another person, and every dream you created together has suddenly disappeared, along with that person. And it infuriates me to think that people believe it is okay to weigh the different forms of pain against each other.

This does not decrease one's pain. Telling a parent that their suffering is the worst, the most unimaginable, the most horrific, does not somehow make it less awful. They are pointless words. And at the same time they are damaging words, as what they do is alienate and dismiss all other forms of grief as not being as significant. I have had to bite my tongue on more than one occasion, as people who were well meaning at times, and at others simply lashing out in their own pain, have made comments that if I had to go through pain, at least it was my husband and not a child; or that it is a blessing I do not have to suffer the ongoing pain that Cam's parents will be forced to endure. I am not sure what makes people think that there is an expiration date on other forms of grief, or that the loss of Cam has not impacted me in such a way that I will forever be changed.

I ask each and every one of you reading this to please never make any kind of comparison about grief. Do not put one type of grief on a pedestal as being more catastrophic than the next. And do not try to console someone by comparing it to something you think would be worse, as this only makes them feel that they do not have the right to feel the unbelievable pain they are actually feeling. Loss is loss, pain is pain, and grief is grief. We deal with it differently and each of us feels it differently, regardless of the type. Until we stop competing we will never allow ourselves to begin healing and supporting each other.

Chapter Twenty-Four:
Abandonment

Is it that my presence is too painful because it reminds
you of his absence? Is it that my laugh reminds you that
it's no longer his jokes I'm laughing at? Does the mere
sight of me remind you of all you've lost?

By Elizabeth Leanne

After Cam died, I took solace in the fact that I was not the only one who had lost an amazing person. There were many who had not even realized how they would be affected by his death. And there were those of us who knew and dreaded it, dreaded the void it would inevitably leave in our hearts and lives. Yet somehow that hole was a little smaller when in the company of others who loved him; to know I was not alone in my suffering; to feel connected to him by their mere presence. It eased the pain, even if only a little.

Then slowly things began to change, life began to either return to normal for some, or to settle into a new routine that did not include Cam, and consequently myself. This secondary loss of connections was not something I was prepared for, and it hurt more than I ever could have imagined.

People who had been a regular part of my life, who I had learned to tolerate, like and even love, suddenly began to drift away. Parties and get-togethers would happen without me being invited; with me hearing of them later. Annual events Cam and I had gone to for years, things we had done with others continued without him, me, or us. It was as if I did not exist outside the unity of Cam and Leanne; as if I alone was not enough to include.

How do I let people know I was not ready for so much of my life to change? That losing Cam was awful enough; I couldn't stand the thought and reality that I was losing so many connected to him too. How do I tell others of the pain their absence is causing me, without seeming overly needy? Without worrying that if they begin to invite me again it will only be out of guilt or obligation?

So, I hold my tongue. I cry behind closed doors. I wonder if they ever liked or cared about me at all, or if they simply tolerated me for Cam. And I really hope it's not me; that it's not because I'm not good enough all on my own to be in their lives, but rather that it simply is too hard to include me; that I remind them that it's all of us who lived, but Cam didn't. If that is the reason, then I take pity on them. I understand their distance. It still hurts, but I know the need to protect oneself from more pain. And if that is what they are doing, then I can honor it. But I fear it may not be, and that loss, the haunting unknown reason behind this so very real and painful loss, is so hard to face.

I grieve not only for him; not only for my best friend, my love and husband, but for the life we had together. For the life we worked hard to create and maintain, the life we dreamed of and began to bring into reality. I grieve for all that was and all that never will be. I grieve because nothing is the same anymore. Yes, the world continues to turn, the sun still rises and others' lives appear to go on unchanged, but for me things have been altered and I, at the center of it all, have been changed. I do not put a value on this change; I simply acknowledge it and grieve it.

In many ways, I'm sure all of this has and will make me stronger, but growth is not without pain and sacrifice. I sit here and grieve the naivety that I used to have the luxury of having. I sit here and look at my phone contact list and realize how long it has been since I saw some of the familiar names flash upon my phone's screen. I wonder if I should reach out, wonder if they would smile at the sight of my name or groan with conflicting feelings of obligation and annoyance. So I put my phone down. I wonder why once again they haven't called, wonder why they didn't respond to my last calls or texts, wonder how it is that I could be so disposable, wonder how long it will be before I stop yearning for them to include me in their lives as they once did.

I likely will never know or understand why they pulled away; it is only speculation and I'm too afraid to reach out and ask; don't trust that they would tell me the truth even if I did. I grieve the loss of my life, my friends and my family, for that is what many of them had become. Many that were there before Cam remain and a few special ones have stayed loyally by my side through all of this, have even called me Cam's greatest gift to them. And there is not a moment that goes by where I am not immensely grateful for each of them, where I also see them as his gifts to me.

Yet, it doesn't change the bitter sadness and feeling of loss, at all the friends and family that had belonged to him and I had adopted as my own for the last number of years. They say people come into our lives for a reason, a season or a lifetime. I just never knew it would be so hard to accept the category so many people fell into.

Chapter Twenty-Five: Another Goodbye

You would think I would be happy to say goodbye to 2014. It would make sense that I would want nothing more than this year of loss and pain to be over with. Alas, I sit here on the last day of 2014 and I just want the seconds to slow down a little, just want to drag the day out. I don't want it to strike midnight, don't want all the cheer and hugs that "Happy New Year" brings. For as soon as that happens, which I know it will in a matter of hours, then it will be a new year, a year in which Cam has never walked this earth.

So yes, 2014 marks the year I lost the love of my life, the year in which I prayed more prayers than I have in my entire life, the year in which I screamed and cried with such ferocious sorrow I thought surely it would kill me, desperately wanted it to kill me. 2014 will forever be etched in my heart; on the timeline of my heart it is the darkest and deepest scar, one I wish I did not have and yet there it is.

So why do I desperately want to stay in 2014 if it has held so much pain and loss? For so many reasons. It is the last year my darling Cam laughed, it is the last year we watched TV together, it is the last year I held him in my arms and felt the warmth of his body begin to warm my cold fingers and toes, it is the last year I felt him hold me and felt safe in his arms, it was the last year I heard his voice, smelt his scent, argued, kissed, watched him sleep, experienced life with him. It was the last year I ever heard the words "I love you, you're my rock, world and reason for living."

It was his last year and the year that marked the end of our life together on earth, and marked the beginning of our more spiritual relationship. It was a year of endings, beginnings and transformations. It was a year like no others before it and I pray I have no others like it in my future. And in a few hours it will be over. In a few hours, I can no longer simply say that my husband passed away earlier this year. No, from now on it will be that he passed away in 2014, a different year, a separate year, a year of the past. And yet it still feels so fresh. It doesn't feel so long ago he asked me to rest my head on his chest and listen to his heart, listen to ensure that it sounded fine. It wasn't that long ago that he loved and trusted me more than any of the devices hooked up to him that were meant to ensure we knew if something was wrong with his heart. That he somehow believed that I was powerful enough to hear the inconsistencies in his heart before the monitor.

It wasn't that long ago when I tried to memorize the sound of his heart beating, of the way I paid attention to the little skip that happened every 3 to 5 seconds. It wasn't long ago that I teased him that he was so in love with me that his heart permanently skipped a beat. It wasn't that long ago that I felt such gratitude at being the person this amazing man chose to spend the last of his days with. Felt such protection over him and determination to do everything in my power, no matter how much it exhausted me, to take care of him. So while it still feels so raw and fresh, suddenly it will have been a different, separate year.

I will be stepping into 2015 without him, doing my first New Year's in six years without my best friend and, quite frankly, I don't want to. But life hasn't really asked me what I want, and the clock keeps ticking, and tomorrow will come regardless of how I feel. 2014 will always be the most bittersweet year of my life. I learned more about myself and the strength of the human spirit this year than I ever wanted to know. I did what I didn't think I could; I survived without Cam and in many ways I flourished. Not because he was gone, but simply because I was determined not to give up on myself or go back on all the promises I made him.

I met new people, made new friends, opened my heart, took chances and fell in love with myself and others. I accomplished things I never expected to and was moved time and time again by people's kindness and desire to make a difference. I have no resolutions other than to continue taking care of me, in whatever way that looks on any given day. And yet my one prayer for myself is that 2015 is a gentler year, one that it is uneventful and possibly slightly boring, that healing continues and peace in my heart becomes the norm.

Chapter Twenty-Six:
And I Survived

The grieving process is like nothing I expected, nothing I or anyone else could prepare for, no matter how long you know it is coming. It steals your breath at the most awkward and inopportune moments. It leaves you numb, feeling disconnected from yourself and the world around you, as if you are simply watching everything happen, without actually being a participant. Time stops and everything begins to be referenced from the time your loved one died.

There is the time before he died and the time after, life has permanently been separated by this event. "Two weeks ago I did…Oh, I mean two weeks before Cam died," was a standard way I told stories and held reference. You die when they die, or at least a part of you does, the part of you that functions, that has control, that feels joy, the part that is alive dies. Or at least that's what happened to me. I have had more panic attacks and grabbed at my throat as I felt it closing than I can count. Each time wondering if this time it would finally be the end, if it would actually allow this pain to just end, if I could join him again, because I was so uninterested in living the potentially long life that was left for me to face.

But no, I never actually stopped breathing; just struggled, gulped for air, covered my mouth to try and stop the hyperventilating. Pulled off the road when driving and parked when it got bad, so I didn't hurt anyone else with my crazy antics. I would sit in my car or house when my dogs were out with the dog walker and scream, and scream and scream till there was nothing left and my throat was raw.

I have cried more tears than I thought humanly possible, quiet ones that slip down my cheeks catching me off guard and quickly wiped away before anyone noticed, or at times that I simply allowed to run while I stared off in space and remembered what it was like, not all that long ago, when he, when Cam, was here; when I could touch him and be touched, when I knew I could call his phone at any time and hear his voice, when he was my everything. Tears that caught in my throat, that flowed so fast and in such a quantity I was sure they would drown me. Sobs shaking my body, leaving me a quivering mess.

I have questioned thousands of times why this had to be his story, my story. Why this one? What lesson am I to learn from this? What if I don't learn it properly and have to be shown again? Will I be able to handle more heartbreak? Life is not fair, I know that very well, and thus feel terrified of what else is in store and how in the hell I can cope with anything else.

I would give anything to have him back, anything to have a different story to write. But I know I can't bring him back, no one can. He is gone, at least physically. I'm alone and single, with a long life ahead of me. And I'm tired of being so sad, I'm tired of feeling drained and as if I can't go on. I'm tired of crying every day, I'm tired of either being devastated or shutting off my feelings.

I want to be happy again. I believe I can and will be happy again. I need to know this is possible. I am still alive, no idea how, but I am, and I have to face that. It is important to remember to be appreciative of it; otherwise, it is a gift that will be wasted. I promised Cam so many times that I would not give up on life, that I would go out there and live fully no matter how that looked or what that meant.

I remember the first day I did not cry. I felt happy, simply happy, like suddenly life was palatable and actually something to look forward to with excitement. What a concept! And then just when I thought I really had gone through the worst of the grief and would be fine, a new wave took me out and it took me out hard.

Once again, I was left a shaky crying mess wondering if I would get back to happy, wondering how long I will go back and forth.

There is no way to know how long the waves will come, or how long any of them will last. All I can do is swim when they hit, let the pain and sadness wash over me and remember it won't always feel so horrible. I expect that there will not be a time in my life where I do not remember him with longing, with complete love and where I do not miss him. But those feelings will not, and are not, paralyzing me any longer. I am slowly but surely embracing life and joy again. Happiness is beginning to take up more room than pain, most days at least.

I still miss him more than I thought humanly possible, and adore him and everything we had, but it isn't quite as bitter a pain. I'm thankful for all we had, for the experience of it and now I want to go out and make my life amazing just like I promised I would. I actually am excited to start dating and flirting, to start investigating what my future might be, what I want it to be. Guilt is something I have tried to avoid and usually do a good job. I refuse to judge myself for the fact that I feel ready to start another chapter far sooner than I had expected, or than I fear is 'socially acceptable'. I know how much I love Cam and that me wanting to find someone else to spend the night, day or however long with has nothing to do with how much I love him. It only has to do with still being alive, and having a body that has needs and a spirit that has decided that life is too short to waste any more time being sad while denying myself simple joys; and human connection is one of those joys.

I cleaned out the rest of his clothes from my closet, yes MY closet, and slept naked for the first time in MY bed since Cam died, something that shows me that I'm getting comfortable in this skin of mine again (See Appendix Six). I'm reclaiming my space and body for me. I switched my wedding rings to my right hand and his to my left middle finger after reading that widows often remove their rings when they realize the rings hold memories and meaning in regards to all that was, but in reality no longer represent what they were meant to.

One day I plan to have our rings combined into one ring for me to wear on my right hand, and I trust I'll know when the time is right. I am no longer married, I'm widowed and single. That word is still bitter in my mouth, I still shiver at it. I laugh bitterly that I was widowed before I was 30. But I can't hold onto yesterday, I want to live in today and look forward to tomorrow, so it was time to move the rings over, to clean out the closet and make room for myself and whoever else may come into my life.

I know I will have setbacks again and again, as that is how this grieving process goes; it is hard, then tolerable, then unimaginable, but I'm not scared of the hard days to come. I will get through them. I got through being a caregiver and watching the love of my life slowly die in front of me, slowly get weaker and disappear.

I watched our marriage change, our dynamic shift in ways I never wanted or imagined. I watched as destiny cheated us. And I survived. And then I watched as my darling Cam died numerous times in front of me. I watched as he came back and then died again and I loved him through it all. And I survived. I watched as he finally left this earth for the final time, and I held him for the last time, kissed his cold skin and walked away, even though it ripped my heart into a thousand pieces. And somehow I survived. I planned a funeral, thanked people, began to write this book and put energy into fundraisers so that maybe one day others have a different story to tell. I fell apart and pulled myself back together. And I survived. I did whatever it took to just get through the day and then the next.

I will never judge myself for what I did or said in order to survive, because if you have not walked this path, and I pray for your sake you haven't, then you have no right to judge. You have no idea. But I do and I survived. I know it is possible to survive the unimaginable. To find your way again, to reclaim who you were, to laugh and I mean really, really laugh again. While I would give anything to have him back and would have continued caring for him forever if I could, I realize that I was far more exhausted than I even realized and I wouldn't have been able to care for him as I had been doing for much longer.

So, while I wanted to keep going, wanted to keep him forever, he made that difficult decision for me, that enough was enough and to just go home. To let me have my life again, to be young and free from a life we so often associate with the elderly. We were each other's everything. But now it's time I love me and put my energy towards taking care of me and this life of mine. You know why? Because I still have a whole other story to tell, a book that has yet to be written. One that inevitably will have heart-break, many lessons and tons and tons of joys, love and laughs, because that is life. I survived and will continue to survive.

I chose, and it is a choice, to embrace life and just go for it, to be excited; and while I look back on all we had fondly, and with longing, I also feel grateful that this chapter is done. Not that he is gone. No, I'll always wish that wasn't our fate; but he is no longer sick, I am no longer living in daily fear of what the next day will bring, of fearing how I will survive without him, and when I'll be expected to try. I am grateful that I am no longer having my heart destroyed every day, at being helpless to save the person I love most in the world and am doing everything humanly possible to make the transition as painless and joyful as possible, all while stuffing my anger, fear, sadness and bitter disappointment.

I'm grateful that I survived. It was long and it was hard, and at the same time it was fast and immobilizing. But I survived. I would never wish what I endured, what Cam endured, on anyone, but if you find yourself there, you will survive. You don't need to know how but you will, trust me. All things come to an end; the beautiful, the devastating. They all end. And you will survive, just as I have. I promise.

Chapter Twenty-Seven: Learning To Live Again

After a loved one dies, there is the decision, and it is just that, regarding whether you will stay alive or join your loved one. Do not underestimate the power or importance of this decision, or think that once the decision is made, it is final. No, it is a daily, sometimes hourly decision to keep going, to endure indescribable pain, exhaustion and heart wrenching loneliness.

It is a decision to resist every instinct that simply longs to be with your partner, to do whatever it takes to end this suffering. Your fight or flight instincts kick in, and yet there is no escape; if you choose to live, then it is a choice to face the pain and endure. Once you begin to make the decision, or should I say continuous decisions, to stay alive, then you are faced with the decision of exactly how you will live. In many cases, we cannot control the events that life presents us with, we cannot control the pain we are asked to endure. However, we do have the ability to choose how we will react to it, and if it will help us grow or leave us bitter.

As I began to wrap my head around the idea of staying in this world without Cam, I realized very quickly that I did not want him to die in vain. He had been terrified that I would take my own life after he died or that his death would destroy me, and while I may have continued to have a heartbeat, it would have been of a broken heart that withdrew and shut out others from fear of future loss. These fears of his were not unfounded. I realized, however, that if I shut others out, if I chose to simply go through the motions for the next 60 years until I too could leave this earth, then all the teachings Cam provided me with would be for nothing.

He had been a catalyst for change in mine and many others' lives. How could I throw that all away? How could I not honor him and all he gave me? It was during these decisions that I had to make that I decided to listen to my friends, and family regarding writing a book in which I told Cam's and my story. As I began to read dozens of books written about grieving or by widows/widowers, I realized how comforting it could be to hear another's story and to know I was not alone. And so I decided that if I could offer that comfort to someone else who didn't know how to go on, someone else who was trying to make the decision whether to stay or join their lost love one, then it would mean that all my suffering and all of Cam's suffering would not be for naught. I decided and continue to decide each day that I will fully embrace life with all of its incredible joys as well as devastating pain. I decided to live, endure and grow.

Making the decision is the first and continuous step. Without it, nothing else is possible. If you do not decide to embrace life and fully live, then all of the next steps do not matter, as you will not need them. Living fully, in spite of the constant longing for someone you will never have again, is not for the faint of heart, as it is not a simple task. However, it is possibly the most rewarding one I have ever experienced. Being a family counsellor, I strongly believed in the power of counselling even when there was nothing the counsellor could do to change my circumstances. Having someone I trusted that was able to witness the trials and tribulations of my caretaking and grieving journey was more valuable to me than I can describe.

From the time that Cam was diagnosed with cancer, until the week before the one year anniversary of his death, I went to counselling on a weekly to monthly basis depending on how badly I was struggling. It was my time to be fully unfiltered and honest. I did not have to be strong or positive. I did not have to worry that the raw intensity would be too much for my counsellor to handle or add to their own struggles.

I had to force myself to remember the things I enjoyed doing both on my own before Cam and I had started dating, as well as together as a couple. And then it was time to decide what the new me, this new freshly exposed, amazingly strong, and yet delicate me, would enjoy having in her life. I would be lying if I said that doing many of these activities in the beginning were enjoyable or easy, because they were neither.

I did my first yoga class three weeks after Cam passed and cried the entire time. I loved yoga before Cam and had regularly attended classes prior to us dating, as well throughout our entire relationship until he became too sick to attend. Cam had initially begrudgingly joined me and then fell in love with it too, and together we put hours upon hours on our mats. I could feel him and yet was acutely aware that he was not there, that he would never join me physically in a yoga class again. But forcing myself to do the moves, even with tears streaking down my cheeks, I opened my body up and the sorrow that was stored in many of my muscles began to be released, which was overwhelming but cleansing. And when I returned the following week, it was a little easier.

I still occasionally get teary in yoga when I remember the pride he had when he managed to master certain poses; when he did his first perfect headstand. I'm okay with crying in public. I thank my body for growing and pushing itself and remember with adoration the absolute strength Cam's body held until the last few months. Slowly all the things that I enjoyed historically, both on my own and with Cam, became easier to do, filled me with more enjoyment. Some I have chosen to let go of. I miss them, but at this time they are simply too hard without him and that's okay.

The main things that I love, our dogs, the gym, yoga, drumming, hiking, biking, running, watching Netflix and drinking peppermint tea are among the joys that we either did together or on my own before I lost him, and they continue to sustain me now. I found me again, I found what brings me joy and I made a decision to ensure those elements are a part of my constant life and routine.

Our bodies and minds are interesting things. Even though you can be grieving with every ounce of your body, old instinctual longings and desires still pop up. I was surprised and in a way horrified with how quickly my sex drive returned after Cam died. I felt too vulnerable to act on it, was beyond terrified that I would burst into tears the first time I had sex with someone else. Yet, the urge and longing was there. Cam had made me promise him that I would not let my dreams die with him. I had always wanted to get married, have children, dogs and own a home. When Cam and I fell in love I assumed it would all be with him, and other than having his children, all of my dreams did come true; it just wasn't for as long as we had hoped. They were my dreams before him, and would remain my dreams after him even though they were tainted with intense fear that they may not all come true.

I made a conscious effort, and man, was it an effort, to not allow my fear of how others would react or their possible judgements limit me from following my heart. I had no way of knowing when or if I would be ready to date, but I couldn't stand being alone and my heart, even when broken, was overflowing with love I wanted to share. Beginning to date was in many ways a horrible process. They were not Cam and he was all I wanted. Every time I sat across from another person all of the ways they were drastically different from him came slamming into me like bricks being dropped from a ten story building. I cried uncontrollable sobs that raked my entire body for four hours straight after my first date with, I'm sure, a very nice guy who just was not the love of my life.

But the next time someone asked, I said yes again. I refused to give up on my promise to Cam that I would not shut myself off from love, and if I didn't go on all the random dates, then how could I ever find someone I might be interested in spending my time with? It felt hopeless at times, felt that I had used my good luck dating card up and been luckier than many and found my soul mate, only to lose him, and was now destined to be alone forever. But I kept saying yes, if only so that I didn't have to sit in my house alone. Most did not get a second date and none got a third, until I met Kelsey. And finally all the flops I had gone on paid off and I can only say thank you to Cam for forcing me to promise that I would get out there and be open to another chance at happiness, life and love.

I got my second chance; a wish come true. I found someone who not only loves me, but respects the journey I am still on. A man who is not threatened by my love for Cam or the tears that still flow at the loss of him. A man who fully accepts me and my history. Accepts my story.

He is not Cam, nor will he ever be. I fell in love with Kelsey for who he is, as his own separate amazing person. He will never replace Cam, no one could, that is not his purpose and not why I have him in my life. But he makes me smile and laugh. He reminds me that my life did not stop when Cam's did, even though there were many days I wish it had. I have learned to dream again and found someone who is worth risking my heart for. I'm in love and so very grateful to experience the amazingness that goes along with being in love.

And Cam remains a central part of our lives for at this time there is no separating my story from his as we are bound together, and thankfully Kelsey understands and accepts this. We still celebrate both of Cam's and my wedding anniversaries and Kelsey will occasionally buy things that he knows, from my stories, will remind me of Cam. I often laugh that I have a love triangle except one of the players is in Heaven.

Not a day goes by where I am not appreciative of this second chance; that my fear of potential future pain did not stop me from opening my heart to the possibility of love; that Cam unselfishly told me he wanted me to love again so I now have no guilt and know for certain he is smiling at me saying, "You go darling, I'm so proud of you."

Falling in love again has not wiped the pain away, but it has made it palatable. It has not changed how much I miss Cam, but I am no longer lonely or struggling to do everything on my own. It has reminded me that we can never know what our future holds or how quickly it can change in devastating, as well as incredible, ways. And while a scary concept, it is also one I will be eternally grateful for.

When I look back on my life, on my story, which I'm still writing every day, I want to be able to answer the question "Did you love fully?" with a full heartedly and truthful "YES!" This is my life goal, this is my sustenance, it is this that forces me out of bed on the days the pain feels unbearable, and motivates me to never give up. I want to love and love well. Even if that means taking the risk of hurting again, for love is truly the only adventure worth living for. In losing Cam, in losing myself, in losing my everything, I found my purpose and I seized the opportunity to create myself all over again, to pick up the pen and begin to write with abundant love the next part of my story. Will you join me? I promise it is worth the risk.

It is hard to imagine that my life with Cam will simply be a chapter in my life;

an extremely important, influential and forever moving chapter, but just a chapter.

I know this to be true as I have had other chapters in this short life of mine,

but, for now, it is hard to imagine how it can possibly ever be just a chapter,

when it still feels like the entire story.

Epilogue:
A Second Chance At Happiness

I watch the sleeping form of my one year old daughter on the baby monitor and once again am struck with the realization of how quickly life can shift and change in wonderful and devastating ways. That change is truly our only guarantee. But, this time I couldn't be happier for this fact, because it means that I was granted my wish, Cam's wish for me, a second chance at happiness. My perfect wish come true, my baby, my little girl. Winter Cameron was born on March 3, 2018 making Kelsey and I beyond proud parents.

I carry my life with Cam, our story, with me. It is not something I desire to move on from or "get over" for it has helped shape who I am and how I interact in this world, as have my many other life experiences. My love for him will carry on forever; however, I realized when I met Kelsey, my life truly did not stop when Cam's did.

Kelsey and I were married on June 19, 2016 in Waterton Park on the rocky shore of Cameron Bay (total coincidence, believe it or not). It was a crazy windy day in which everyone in attendance, including ourselves, wore onesie pajamas instead of formal wear. I loved Kelsey and was excited to marry him, but I struggled with the idea of walking down the aisle in another white dress. We talked of eloping, of doing a destination wedding, of all kinds of ways that we could fulfill the desire to be married to each other without the risk of a bitter taste being left in my mouth on that important day if memories of the previous times I walked down the aisle came back to me.

I wanted this day to be ours, to be different, to be separate and to be special. While sitting on our couch, I joked we could just wear onesies and, without hesitating, Kelsey latched onto the idea and quickly started brainstorming how he could have a cane and top hat, which indeed he did. He also surprised me on the day by wearing the same shoes Cam had worn to both of our weddings, to honor the man who loved me enough to set me free to love again.

Similarly, I wore my veil which I had also worn at my and Cam's previous two weddings, as well as a fanny pack filled with flowers. Yes, you read that correctly, I wore a fanny pack down the aisle! My florist stated she had never been given such a strange request as to create a bouquet of flowers in a fanny pack for a bride to wear; however, this was necessary as my hands were full holding my dogs leashes as they and my parents walked (or excitedly dragged) me toward my future husband. After the ceremony and some pictures, everyone changed into formal gear, at which point I did wear a white wedding dress, for more pictures and an epic dance party under a full moon illuminating the mountains surrounding Waterton Townsite. I had the tie Cam had worn at our butterfly wedding sewn into the underside of my wedding dress and his tie from our first wedding was wrapped around the stems of the bouquet of flowers I had for the reception and pictures, since a fanny pack just didn't provide the right feel with a wedding dress.

Kelsey has understood, respected and supported the process I need to take in remembering and loving Cam. Together we have created traditions to honor Cam and assist my healing journey. Every Christmas since Cam has passed we have made birdseed decorations in the shapes of Christmas trees, stars, stockings and gingerbread men, which we then take to his bench in Kananaskis on Christmas Day in order to decorate the trees.

When trying to decide how to celebrate Cam's life on February 15th that very difficult first anniversary, it was Kelsey who suggested we watch a Disney animation movie and eat Cam's favorite foods, spicy pizza with Franks Red Hot Sauce, hot chicken wings, Twix, and Cheezies. These traditions do not eliminate the pain of missing Cam; rather, they allow me to focus on something else while bringing moments of joy and laughter. Both Kelsey and I look forward to including Winter in these traditions as she grows older and explaining their importance, as well as who Cam was and why we remember him.

I have entered a new chapter in MY story, and it is a truly wonderful and magical one that I'm so happy I stayed around to experience. I would be lying, though, if I said it was a happy ever after, as I do not believe such simplicity of experience exists. Kelsey and I have to work to keep our relationship healthy, and there are hurtles along the way just like in all relationships. I struggle with the all too tempting tendency to compare Kelsey to the perfect version of Cam my memory has put on a pedestal, which is neither fair nor accurate. Kelsey has put hundreds of hours of work into upgrading or changing aspects of our home, but he continues to struggle with the feeling of simply being a guest, of not truly belonging here, that this is my home, or worse Cam's and my home.

One day we will move, we will find a home that is ours and create new, wonderful and, I'm sure, difficult memories there. I know this and try to prepare for it, but for now I am not ready to leave my beautiful "acreage without the work", and luckily Kelsey again understands this. So no, it is not a happy ever after ending, but none of ours ever are. Indeed it is not an ending at all; instead, it is a part of a wonderful story, a story I am living and writing every second of everyday. A story that exists because I learned to soar with burnt wings.

Elizabeth and Kelsey

December 2014 Decorating the trees with
birdseed decorations around Cams plaque for Christmas.

Tribute meal to Cam's passing every February 15.

Every year since 2015 at Christmas Elizabeth and Kelsey
decorate the trees around Cam's memorial bench
with birdseed ornaments.
Easier to get to in the snow then his plaque.

June 19, 2016 Dandelion/Onesie Wedding

Part 2 of our wedding – Formal Wear

Beautiful Waterton National Park, Alberta

**Cam's tie from Butterfly Wedding
sewn into the underside of Elizabeth's dress**

**Cam's tie from their 1st wedding
wrapped around Elizabeth's bouquet**

32 weeks pregnant pregnancy photoshoot

So thrilled with this dream come true!

Introducing Winter Cameron

Newborn photoshoot 2 weeks old

6 month photoshoot

18 months old - Better than a wish come true!

Appendix One:
Butterfly Wedding Ceremony

Tribute from Unknown Source read at our wedding

So difficult to define, or even to describe,

love is the most complex of life's experiences.

Love is the essence of all of our relationships; it's the energy that connects us and an intricate part of who we are as human beings.

Love has nothing to do with knowledge, education, or power....

and is beyond behavior.

It's the core of creativity, the fuel of hope, the opposite of fear and ultimately,

it is the only thing we have that we can really give.

Love is present in everyday life; it's in all of our wonderful experiences –

and even in our tragedies.

Love is what gives our days their deep meaning, and gives us the ability to acknowledge the richness and beauty all around us.

Love is what we are made of... and made for.

It is ours for the taking... and ours to give.

We are here today because two people fell in love and have been willing to work hard in order to ensure that love continues to grow.

Many people believe that entering into marriage is the final step in a romantic relationship. As they see it, a couple meets, gets to know each other, falls in love, decides they want to go through life together, and then take the final step—marriage.

But marriage is not meant to be the final step in a couple's relationship—it is really just the beginning of a grand adventure, that hopefully,

will be long and fruitful for each couple.

Marriage deepens and enriches every facet of life.

Happiness is fuller, memories are fresher, commitment is stronger, even anger is felt more strongly, and passes away more quickly.

Marriage understands and forgives the mistakes life is unable to avoid. It encourages and nurtures new life, new experiences, new ways of expressing a love that is deeper than life.

When two people pledge their love and care for each other in marriage, they create a spirit unique unto themselves which binds them closer

than any spoken or written words.

Marriage is a promise made in the hearts of two people who love each other, and the potential of marriage requires a lifetime to fulfill.

Elizabeth and Cam, the first lesson we must learn as a married couple is how to live together with each other. Love is given to us by our family and friends, we learn to love by being loved. Learning to love and learning to live together is one of life's greatest challenges. That is the goal of a married life.

You have shared joys, blessings, and even more challenges than some ever do, in your short time as a married couple. And, today you wish to reconfirm your commitment to working together to make your marriage grow and blossom in the years to come, your commitment to standing together no matter what the future may hold. May this ceremony, renewing the vows you took to become life partners on your wedding day, remind you that despite the stresses which occur, your love, respect, trust and understanding of each other will increase your contentment and heighten your joy in living together.

Please face each other and join hands.

Cam, will you continue to have Elizabeth as your wife and continue to live in this happy and loving marriage?

Cam: I WILL

Do you reaffirm your love for her, and will you love, honor and cherish her in sickness and in health, for richer or poorer, for better for worse, and forsaking all others, be faithful to her for as long as you both shall live?

Cam: I DO

Elizabeth, will you continue to have Cam as your husband and continue to live in this happy and loving marriage?

Elizabeth: I WILL

Do you reaffirm your love for him, and will you love, honor and cherish him in sickness and in health, for richer or poorer, for better for worse, and forsaking all others, be faithful to him for as long as you both shall live?

Elizabeth: I DO

Cam spoke from the heart for his personal vows, but brought me to tears and made me burst out laughing as he described our love and his absolute devotion to me.

My vows:

Cam, last year when we exchanged our wedding vows, it was with the very difficult understanding that no two people can ever know how long their forever will be. While this reality is something everyone knows, I believe that we had a more pressing and intimate understanding of just how important it is to really enjoy every minute we have together. On our wedding day, I pledged to love you in sickness and in health, and for better or worse for as long as we both shall live. I made those vows with the full knowledge that they would be tested. And I renew them again today in front of our family and friends with even more love and commitment, as the trials of the last year have created a new level of intimacy in our relationship. One that I do not believe a couple can have until they face the possible reality of losing each other. Thank you for being my constant reminder of how important it is to live in the moment and for the sometimes not so gentle reminders that worrying about the future is only self-abuse. You bring me more laughter and joy than I could have ever hoped for. And I appreciate that you are always eventually willing to apologize for your actions or words, which hurt me. We have by no means had an easy relationship and we have been tested in nearly every way a couple can; however, our dedication and perhaps Taurus stubbornness, has continued to make this a healthier relationship. I feel that all of our hard work is paying off and have tremendous hope for the future, for our future. I am simply ecstatic that I get to continue life's journey by your side. Once again, I promise to love you, honor you and keep you, for better or worse, in sickness and in health, for as long as we both shall live.

On your wedding day you exchanged rings as a symbol of the never-ending circle of love. Rings serve as a reminder of your wedding vows to each other, and your commitment to live in unity, love and happiness. At this time, it is appropriate to reconfirm the meaning of the rings you wear.

Please join your left hands together so that Cam's hand is on top. Cam, please repeat after me...

Elizabeth, I wear this ring you placed on my hand, as a symbol of my love and commitment to you.

Now, with Elizabeth's hand on top, Elizabeth please repeat after me:

Cam, I wear this ring you placed on my hand, as a symbol of my love and commitment to you.

With this renewed commitment in mind, please exchange the presents you have each gotten for one other. (Since we had already given rings, Cam got me a Pandora bracelet charm that was an engagement ring and wedding band interwoven with 'I love you' engraved on it. And I had bought him a 10 inch hematite inukshuk which was something he had asked me to get him, if I ever saw one years earlier when we had started collecting inukshuks.)

I ask that you each remember to continue to cherish each other as special and unique individuals, and that you each respect the thoughts and ideas of one another. And most of all, be able to forgive each other, and not hold grudges against one another. Live each day in love with each other, always being there to give love, comfort, and refuge to each other, in good times and bad.

Elizabeth and Cam, today you have renewed the promises and vows you made to each other on your wedding day. You have symbolized the renewal of the marriage union by the joining of hands, the taking of vows, by the wearing of your wedding rings and the exchanging of presents.

It is with pleasure that I conclude the ceremony of renewing the vows of marriage that joined you and binds you as husband and wife. Please celebrate this renewal of vows with a kiss!

Appendix Two:
The Regime

<u>Disclaimer</u>: In no way am I claiming to be able to cure cancer or prolong anyone's life. I simply am reporting what Cam and I tried and our experience with it. Please do your own research before trying anything I discuss.

The two books which I found to be instrumental in determining supplements to take and how to move forward after Cam was diagnosed with cancer are *Healing the Gerson Way* by Charlotte Gerson as well as *Embrace Release Heal* by Leigh Fortson. I fully recommend reading these books from cover to cover for anyone faced with a diagnosis of cancer or who loves someone who is making that journey.

It was while reading *Healing the Gerson Way* that I learned about coffee enemas and how they aid in the process of detoxification as well as offer pain relief. Please refer to this book in order to learn why they are effective as well as how to safely do them.

Please visit <u>www.earthing.com</u> in order to learn about Earthing and how Grounding Mats or other products they have help the body to achieve a similar balance to that which occurs when we allow our skin to come into direct contact with the earth. Numerous testimonies can also be found at this site regarding how reconnecting with the earth has allowed people to feel more charged and be healthier.

During my research early on I learned of Structured Water and the benefits it has on our bodies as a whole. Coincidently, my mother became a distributor of Natural Action Technologies which sells various water structuring units. The benefits of structuring water have been found to include neutralizing toxins in the water, increased absorption of nutrients in our food, healthier bodies, dissolves hard minerals in the water, as well as decalcifies the pineal gland. Simply put, water structuring units replicate what we would see in a natural mountain stream, water tumbling over rocks and twisting and turning. This is in stark contrast to the straight pipes we pump water through to our homes which, according to Natural Action Technologies, alters the chemical makeup of the water molecules. For further information, please visit www.naturalaction.com

Appendix Three:
Osho Zen Tarot Cards – The Lovers

Commentary: "What we call love is really a whole spectrum of relating, reaching from the earth to the sky. At the most earthy level, love is sexual attraction. Many of us remain stuck there, because our conditioning has burdened our sexuality with all kinds of expectations and repression. Actually the biggest 'problem' with sexual love is that it never lasts. Only if we accept this fact can we then really celebrate it for what it is – welcome it happening, and say good-bye with gratitude when it's not. Then as we mature, we can begin to experience the love that exists beyond sexuality and honors the unique individuality of the other. We begin to understand that our partner often functions as a mirror, reflecting unseen aspects of our deeper self and supporting us to become whole. This love is based in freedom, not expectation or need. Its wings take us higher and higher towards the universal love that experiences all as one."

The Lovers: "These three things are to be taken note of: the lowest love is sex – it is physical – and the highest refinement of love is compassion. Sex is below love, compassion is above love; love is exactly in the middle. Very few people know what love is. Ninety-nine percent of people, unfortunately, think sexuality is love – it is not. Sexuality is very animal; it certainly has the potential of growing into love, but it is not actual love, only the potential... If you become aware and alert, meditative, then sex can be transformed into love. And if your meditativeness becomes total, absolute, love can be transformed into compassion. Sex is the seed, love is the flower, compassion is the fragrance. Buddha has defined compassion as 'love plus meditation'. When your love is not just a desire for the other, when your love is not only a need, when your love is a sharing, when your love is not that of a beggar but an emperor, when your love is not asking for something in return but is ready only to give – to give for the sheer joy of giving – then add meditation to it and pure fragrance is released. This is compassion; compassion is the highest phenomenon."

Appendix Four:
Ride To Conquer Cancer

Some names have been changed in this article for privacy purposes.

Calgary Herald article: When Elizabeth learned that her fiancé had cancer, her reaction was predictable. "Devastation, shock and horror," she says of the many emotions she felt. "But after months of not knowing, it was almost a relief. That relief vanished once we learned what kind of cancer it was." After months of pain and discomfort, doctors told Cam he was suffering from an extremely rare and far-progressed sarcoma called spindle cell cancer and likely had only months to live. Not long after receiving the devastating news, the young couple did something far less predictable: they made their commitment official with not one, but two weddings. "A wedding is a wonderful way to celebrate a life and love," says Elizabeth of the husband who took his last breaths this past February. "You learn how important those vows are, especially when it comes to in sickness and in health."

On Saturday, the 30-year-old will celebrate her husband once more when she hops on her bike to participate in the Enbridge Ride to Conquer Cancer (www.conquercancer.ca), a 200-kilometre, two-day annual cycling event that raises funds for cancer research. "Last year, Cam went for a walk and saw the riders near our home in Black Diamond," says Elizabeth, a member of the Tom Baker Cancer Conquerors, a team that has already raised more than $380,000 towards a $500,000 fundraising goal. "He was so inspired by it, he said he wanted to ride in it one day." That dream would never be realized for the young man who became one of her best friends while the two were Junior High students at Calgary's Foothills Academy. "He was the funniest person I've met in my entire life," she says of her then future husband. "He was quick witted but also very kind." After graduation, the two went their separate ways, but later reconnected as adults. This time, they realized the warmth of their friendship came with fireworks and soon were planning a wedding for the summer of 2013.

There was, though, a cloud hanging over their happy lives. "Cam had been feeling sick for months and was going back and forth to the doctor's," says Elizabeth of her husband, who was finding walking painful. "They kept saying he must have pulled something and just needed muscle relaxants." The truth was that Cam had tumors in his heart and skeletal structure. "We decided it wasn't going to take away our dreams," says Elizabeh, who quickly assembled family members for an intimate wedding on Sept. 2, 2012, less than two weeks after his diagnosis. When Cam went into remission the following spring, Elizabeth decided they would also go ahead with the bigger wedding they had been planning. "The first wedding was desperate and sad, but for the second we were feeling that maybe we beat it," she says of her June 2013 nuptials. "We were feeling very hopeful." That hope translated into buying a new home in Black Diamond and beginning fertility treatments to conceive a child.

The joyful reprieve was just that: by October of last year, the cancer had come back, this time with 30 new tumors in his brain. In early January of this year, Cam went into cardiac arrest four times; when he was revived, he said he wasn't ready to go because he hadn't properly said goodbye to his wife. After yet another day of horrifying cardiac arrests on Valentine's Day, he died at age 28 just after midnight. "We said everything we had to say to each other," she says of conversations both joyful and painful. "Together, we learned about the true meaning of love." Over the past few months, the young widow has found solace in long rides on her bike, training for the Ride to Conquer Cancer. "I don't think I've had one cry-free ride," says Elizabeth, who works as a family counsellor, in addictions and mental health. Participating in the fundraising ride will bring a roller-coaster of emotion, she adds. But the months of training have been therapeutic for her grieving journey. "This is not just training for a bike ride," she says. "The last two years I dedicated my life to Cam and I'm grateful that I could be there for him. This ride is for him, but it is also for me."

Appendix Five:
Ultimately My Choice

Fairly early on in my relationship with Kelsey, I broached the topic of still holding rights to Cam's sperm and that I was torn on my feelings around potentially not using it to have a child. Many of my fears around a future partner taking offense or seeing this as evidence around loving Cam more than them luckily did not come to fruition. Rather, Kelsey offered empathy around this decision and maintained from the first time we discussed it until I had finally made my decision that it was my decision alone to hold onto the sperm; if that allowed me to feel connected to Cam, then he supported it. He, however, was not open to us using Cam's sperm to have a child and raise as our own. Rather than it being an issue of jealousy, Kelsey explained that he worried about the genetics that would be passed onto our child if we were to use Cam's sperm. We discussed on different occasions the potential risk that a child born of Cam's sperm could possibly be more predisposed to cancer, and was this a risk we were willing to take? Kelsey wasn't. It was so much more complicated than that for me.

It wasn't until Kelsey and my daughter, Winter, was a few months old that I was able to come to a decision. Through multiple discussions with friends and gallons of tears, I decided to fill out the paperwork required to dispose of the stored sperm. I had hoped to be able to donate it for someone else to use; but their policies did not allow this. A friend of mine helped me explore how Winter would potentially interpret my actions if I chose to move forward and have a baby with Cam's sperm. It likely would have meant the end of my marriage with Kelsey, her father. Would she wonder if I loved this other child more than I loved her, because I was willing to leave my relationship with her father to have one with a man who no longer is alive? The possibility that Winter would question if this hypothetical child was more important than her, given the extent I would have to go to and what would be given up to have it, made my answer clear. Winter is my dream come true. She carries Cameron's name and that is enough.

Appendix Six:
Reclaiming My Space

An excruciating part of the grieving process is figuring out what to keep and what to let go of. And yet, it is essential and unavoidable. There is no time line around when to do this and I think, like much of the grieving process, it is dependent on the person and who it is they lost. I began going through his clothes and belongings three weeks after he had passed. Initially it was to distribute his belongings to others who had loved and lost him so they too could have things that reminded them of him. His jackets and snowboarding gear was given to friends who wanted it. Certain jewelry or sentimental items went to family members. Once I realized that in order to afford to keep my home, I would need to open the doors to roommates. A new pressure was applied to clean out his things and create space. This was a much more painful process and I felt angry and resentful at being forced to let go of things sooner than I was ready, but out of necessity.

I created four piles: "donate", "sell", "unsure" and "keep". In many ways I was ruthless in this process. I have always been one to let go of sentimental things if it was not of use and this was a skill that came in very handy at this time. His workout equipment, electronics and music equipment were sold, which we had agreed upon prior to his passing. Most of his clothes I brought to a homeless shelter knowing that they would be appreciated and well used. I did hold onto two of my favorite soft t-shirts of Cam's, (which I still will wear as pajama tops), four of his sweaters that I often wore more than he did, as well as his warmest winter jacket that I love to use for dog walks when it is below -25 degrees Celsius. I kept and treasure all of the cards, notes, poems and drawings we had done for each other both when friends and as a couple. His wallet and all his ID's along with the gear shift off his truck were also items I could not part with. All of these items fit in two boxes, which I keep in my shed. I haven't looked at them since sorting them. It is reassuring to know they are there, but I haven't been ready to walk down memory lane yet. Again, being ruthless, I really struggled with whether or not to keep his wedding shoes. It felt like a waste to leave them in a box never to be enjoyed again; however, as with so many items, memories slammed into me when I looked at them and I couldn't bring myself to let them go. Knowing all this, Kelsey surprised me by wearing them at our wedding, thus making them even more special to me. His housecoat still hangs on our bedroom door and Kelsey often uses it now, something that I'm always surprised doesn't bother him. The Inukshuks that Cam and I collected over the years still can be seen throughout Kelsey and my home. I will never see an Inukshuk without smiling, without thinking of Cam, without taking a big breath and knowing, as always, he is still guiding me home.

Appendix Seven:
Time Line

1984 – May 3rd Elizabeth Leanne was born in Regina, Saskatchewan Canada

1985 – May 11th Cameron Charles was born in Calgary, Alberta Canada

1986 - Elizabeth and her parents moved to Dawson City, Yukon Canada

1994 – Elizabeth diagnosed with a learning disability and moved with her parents to Calgary, Alberta Canada in order to attend Foothills Academy, a private school for children with learning disabilities. Her father traveled back and forth between the Yukon and Alberta.

1996 – Elizabeth's parents divorced. Her dad returned to the Yukon full time.

1998 – Cam started at Foothills Academy. Met Elizabeth who went by Leanne at that time.

2000 – Cam left Foothills Academy to go to a public high school.

- Elizabeth's half-brother was born and lived with her dad and new step-mom.

2002 – Elizabeth graduated High School and started postsecondary school at Mount Royal College in Calgary, Alberta Canada to get her Social Work Diploma.

- Elizabeth's half-sister was born and lived with her dad, step-mom and brother.

2003 – Cam graduated High School.

2004 – Cam moved to Fredericton, New Brunswick Canada to attend Recording Arts School.

2005 – Elizabeth's youngest half-sister was born and lived with her dad, step-mom and siblings.

- Elizabeth graduated from College and began working as a Youth Worker.
- Cam moved to Kelowna, British Columbia Canada to continue his Recording Arts School.

2007 – Elizabeth moved to Victoria, British Columbia to attend the University of Victoria to take her Bachelors of Social Work.

- Cam and Elizabeth got Facebook and began talking.

2008 – In the fall, Cam moved back to Calgary, Alberta Canada.

- December 11th Cam and Elizabeth, aka Leanne, reconnected in person.

2009 – Cam started at SAIT in Calgary, Alberta Canada to become an electrician.

- Elizabeth moved to Calgary, Alberta Canada from March till September while off from University to be with Cam and work as a Youth Worker. During this time they broke up and struggled in their relationship due to his drinking.

2010 – April 17th Cam committed to sobriety and Elizabeth supported him by choosing not to drink also.

- Began dating again in a long distance relationship.
- July Elizabeth bought a condo in Victoria, British Columbia Canada.
- August Elizabeth graduated with her Bachelors of Social Work from the University of Victoria.
- September Elizabeth started her Masters of Social Work at the University of Victoria.
- December 3rd became engaged and planned for wedding in 2013.

2011 – August Cam moved to Victoria, British Columbia Canada to live with Elizabeth.

- November first began experiencing pain but dismissed due to thinking it was just a pulled muscle.
- December 11th Got their dog Bentley a Nova Scotia Duck Toller.

2012 – February Cam moved back to Calgary, Alberta Canada with the plan for Elizabeth to follow.

- March Elizabeth put condo up for sale and moved to Calgary, Alberta Canada.
- May Lump on side of neck. Gone on own by the time he got into his doctor.
- Numerous doctors' appointments between February and July due to pain in his bones and at times struggles to walk.
- July 11th Condo had sold. Elizabeth and Cam returned to Victoria to pack it up and put furniture in storage. Noticed a lump on side of Cam's neck.
- July 12th Cam went on fishing trip with his dad on Vancouver Island while Elizabeth stayed with a friend in Victoria.
- July 17th Took furniture out of storage and began trip back to Calgary. Lump on Cam's neck had grown significantly and called to book doctor's appointment.
- July 20th Doctor's appointment in Calgary. Sent to emergency department for further examination.
- July 21st Cam met with Infectious Disease specialist regarding lump on neck. Elizabeth met with a realtor to begin looking for a house to buy.
- July 22nd Cam went for a biopsy of the lump on neck. Elizabeth met with the realtor again to continue looking for homes. Cam called and asked to come to hospital due to getting diagnosis of cancer.
- Early August learned Cam had High Grade Spindle Cell Sarcoma, only 50% survival rate of one year.

- Mid-August began chemotherapy.
- August 22nd Elizabeth and Cam decided not to wait till wedding in 2013 and get married immediately.
- September 2nd Cam and Elizabeth were married in an intimate wedding.
- September 3rd Cam's hair began to fall out due to chemotherapy.
- October 31st Elizabeth completed her Masters of Social Work Program.
- December Cam and Elizabeth visited her family in the Yukon.

2013 – February Elizabeth began working as a Family Counsellor for an Adolescent Addictions and Mental Health unit at a hospital in Calgary.

- May 3rd Cam and Elizabeth purchased a home in Black Diamond, Alberta Canada.
- May 21st Cam was told he no longer needed to do chemotherapy and there was no active cancer cells.
- May 27th Got possession of home in Black Diamond.
- June 10th Moved into home in Black Diamond.
- June 20th Floods in southern Alberta including Black Diamond.
- June 29th Cam and Elizabeth renewed their vows in their Butterfly Wedding in Duncan, British Columbia.
- July 8th Started fostering dogs through ARF and Mickey came to stay with them originally as a foster.
- July 27th Decided to adopt Mickey and continue fostering other puppies.
- September 8th Cam had his first headache.
- September 22nd Naked in Solidarity Elizabeth shaved her head.
- September 27th Found out the cancer had returned throughout Cam's body.
- October 3rd Found out Cam had over 30 tumors in his brain.

- October 9th Elizabeth found out Cam likely only had a few months to live.
- October 10th Elizabeth went on disability leave from work to stay with Cam.
- November 3rd – 10th Elizabeth and Cam went to Mexico with his dad and step-mom.
- November 6th Cam became very ill in Mexico.
- November 10th Cam was admitted to hospital as soon as plane arrived back in Calgary for a week.
- End of November Cam and Elizabeth went to Victoria to visit Elizabeth's dad, step-mom and three siblings who had moved there for the children to attend school.
- December 15th Cam had four grand mal seizures and was hospitalized until December 22nd.

2014 – January 29th Cam had 5 seizures and went into cardiac arrest 3 times. Was hospitalized until February 6th and then sent home.

- February 12th Cam had a seizure and was sent home from the emergency department.
- February 14th Final day together, Cam said goodbye.
- February 15th Cam passed away.
- February 21st Celebration of Life/Funeral.
- February 28th Glenlyon Norfolk School Cut-a-thon.
- August 9th and 10th Ride to Conquer Cancer.
- August 11th First date with Kelsey.

2015 – August 8th and 9th Ride to Conquer Cancer both Kelsey and Elizabeth completed it.

- November 1st Elizabeth got engaged to Kelsey.

2016 – June 19th Elizabeth and Kelsey were married.

2017 – June 24th Found out Elizabeth was pregnant.

2018 – March 3rd Winter was born.

- July Elizabeth decided to let Cam's sperm be destroyed.

Appendix Eight:
A Playlist to Live and Love By

In honor of Cam's love for music, I included some of the songs that were important to us, or spoke to me prior as well as after his death.

- "Everyday Boy" by Joan Armstrong
  - o I first heard this song when I was 16 years old and it initially reminded me of my then infant brother. I have continued to love this song and it will always hold a special place in my heart for my brother, but its lyrics took on a new meaning in relation to Cam shortly after he had been diagnosed with cancer. I can't hear this song without smiling and singing in my very off key voice as loud as I can while thinking about these two 'boys' who hold such an important part of my heart.

- "One that I Want" by Grease Soundtrack
  - o At the Butterfly Wedding, when we said 'I do' and kissed, this song began to play. Cam, myself and the rest of the bridal party danced our way up the aisle listening to it in order to kick off the celebration. It was a perfect fit, since he had shaped up and grown so much in order to be emotionally healthy through sobriety and counselling.

- "Whatever It Takes" by Lifehouse
  - o The first time I heard this song was shorty after returning to Victoria in 2009. I called Cam crying and told him to google the song. It described the conversation we had had hundreds of times around his drinking and the impact on our relationship and why I couldn't be with him while he was drinking. Cam's

matter of fact response was, "Every Lifehouse song describes us." So grateful that finally he really did do whatever it took to turn it all around.

- "It's My Life" by Bon Jovi
  - This was my theme song when I was 16 years old and in the midst of teenage angst. It has continued to help propel me through life especially when my decisions might not align with what has been expected of me. In April 2013, Cam surprised me with tickets and we were able to go and see Bon Jovi in Calgary, Alberta Canada which was simply incredible and a dream come true.

- "Everything" by Lifehouse
  - As previously mentioned, many of Lifehouse's songs described Cam's and my relationship. This one in particular resonated with me on a deep level as he was truly my everything, even when we couldn't be together because of distance or drinking. It was to this song that our wedding party, as well as myself, walked down the aisle at the Butterfly Wedding.

- "I Won't Give Up" by Jason Mraz
  - I walked down the aisle at our first wedding to this song, it was Cam's and my first dance song at the Butterfly Wedding and it played on the slideshow at his funeral. Initially, it was meant to represent not giving up on us, and not giving up on life. However, after he passed, it quickly took on another meaning; a promise to him that I won't give up on myself.

- "I have Nothing" by Whitney Houston
  - My love for Whitney Houston started as a young child after watching The Bodyguard and then learning she, indeed, was a singer. I sang this song into my pretend microphone to an eye rolling Cam far too many times to

count. Often after an argument in an attempt to lighten the mood and remind him how much I loved him, I'd put this on nice and loud and bounce around singing until his beautiful smile lit up his face.

- "For My Broken Heart" by Reba McEntire
  - o I heard this song shortly after Cam had passed and it resonated deeply with how I was feeling, and my experience of trying to keep going when it felt like my world had ended.

- "How Do I Live?" by Trisha Yearwood
  - o I first heard this song in 2013 after Cam had been re-diagnosed with cancer and I knew I would be losing him. It was added to the playlist to listen to if I ever needed to have a good cry, which was extremely often during that period of my life.

- "Unconditionally" by Katy Perry
  - o I adore Katy Perry and Cam would often sing many of her songs along with me. This song was chosen to play during part of the slideshow at his funeral for in the end our love did become unconditional, it surpassed so many trials. Trials I never imagined having to face.

- "Say Something" by A Great Big World
  - o I heard this song on the radio a couple of days after Cam had been declared dead, only to return to life. Up until that point I had been so busy in doctors' meetings and supporting Cam that I hadn't stopped to think about what had happened and how it impacted me. As this song played, the words triggered a flood of memories. It was like watching a movie on fast forward with each image more jarring than the last. I was left sobbing and trying to catch my breath. The rawness of what we had gone through and that, indeed, he did come back to say something, along with

the sickening knowledge that eventually I'd be asked to say goodbye to him all over again.

- "Bittersweet" by Within Temptation

  - Within Temptation was a band we discovered in 2009 and became our theme songs. Loss, heart ache, and longing for what you can't have echoed our struggle of wanting to be together and yet knowing we were toxic for each other at that time. As our relationship got healthier, the relevance of their music decreased in our lives and I forgot all about them until watching the slideshow I made of pictures of us from 2008-2009 when I was moving back to Victoria at the end of the summer. In the slideshow, Bittersweet and Memories are two of the songs the pictures play to. Now that he's gone their songs and their lyrics have a whole new relevance to me.

- "Uneasy" by One Less Reason

  - I heard this song shortly after Cam passed away or at least registered it at that time. The words spoke to me and called me to listen to the song over and over while tears streamed down my face and threatened to choke me.

- "You Make Me Smile" by Blue October

  - While trying to choose songs that represented the chapters and held meaning to me this song came on from my wedding playlist from the Butterfly wedding. Immediately, I had a visceral reaction and was transported back to 2009 when Cam and I would belt out this song at the top of our longs. Later, upon deciding to no longer be together and returning to Victoria, I cried buckets of tears listening to this song on repeat. It was from this song I coined my catch phrase "You make me smile", which I said nearly as often as "I love you."

- "Out There" by Ministry of Sound

  o Cam fell in love with this song when he was still drinking and would often call me and just put the song on without saying anything. As he claimed, it said everything he couldn't. After he died, this song took on a very different meaning for me and represented the emptiness and void I felt. I knew he was somewhere in this universe, felt him close, but he wasn't physically here and that was devastating.

- "Somewhere" by Within Temptation

  o As previously quoted, Within Temptation was our theme band for the summer of 2009. Rediscovering them has brought back many memories, not all of them pleasant as they are from the most tumultuous time in our relationship. As incredibly devastating as loosing Cam to death was, in some ways it was easier to accept than trying to conceive not being together while alive. When he died, I knew he loved me, knew he had done everything to try and stay with me, knew I had done everything I could to keep him just a little longer. There was no option to go back to him. The decision was made for me.

- "Forever's Gone" by Christine Evans

  o Christine Evans is another artist who I turned to through 2009-2010 while struggling to find my footing around loving someone who did not look like I could be with. Many of her songs were on the mixed CD's I made Cam on what was meant to be a goodbye Christmas present in 2009. Like so much of the music that I turned to during the first time my heart broke at the loss of Cam after he died, the songs took on a whole new meaning and intensity.

- "Faraway" by Nickelback

  o Being in a long distance relationship had its many challenges. I have vivid memories of dancing in the living room of Cam's mom's house when I was there visiting to this song. It was our long distance theme song and always made me feel closer to him when I heard it. Three weeks after he passed I went and saw a medium to reach out and talk with Cam. It was an amazing experience and have no question in my mind that, indeed, he was there given the medium knowing things not even my family or closest friends knew. Upon getting into my car and turning it on, this song started and I burst into tears knowing he was reaching out to me, confirming that we were simply in a different kind of long distance relationship, but he was still with me.

- "Memories" by Within Temptation

  - Quite possibly my favorite Within Temptation song and maybe the most depressing. Ironically, after a friend of mine watched the slideshow I made in 2009 in which this song was played, she jokingly stated, "It looks like a funeral video. Who died?" I had never thought of that, but the words of this song and the way it is sung definitely enlists that feeling. Never did I imagine the meaning would become so much more relevant.

- "Dat Baby Don't Look Like Me" by Shawty Putt ft. Lil Jon

  - In our first week together, when it was only meant to be the two of us having fun and then saying goodbye, Cam found this song. We watched the music video and died laughing. Because we are random it was decided that this would officially be "our song". I think we loved that it was as unromantic as they come. By the end of that Christmas trip we knew all the words and would randomly send lyrics to each other over text. Cam's favorite line was, "Now children, what do you say when you meet a nice man?" and I'd write back, "Are you my daddy?" It makes no sense, but that was part of the beauty of it.

- "Recovering" by Celine Dion

  o I first heard this song a few years after Cam had died and it reminded me of the grief journey I was on. How day by day I was reclaiming my life, was learning to love Cam and yet not have that be central to my life as it had been. I was finding me again.

- "Fix You" by Coldplay

  o I do not remember when I first heard this song, but immediately loved it and reminded me of the struggle of realizing that I could not fix him when he was drinking, nor could I fix him while he was dying of cancer. It was not my job to fix him no matter how hard I did try.

- "There You'll Be" by Faith Hill

  o This was another song that made its way onto the CD's I made for Cam when saying goodbye and trying to ensure he knew how much I loved him even if I couldn't be with him while he was drinking. And just like with almost every song that resonated with me during that time, it similarly helped me get through losing him permanently years later.

- "Still Believe in Love" by Jenny Hyun

  o Both Cam and I were huge Twilight fans and went to all but the first movie together in theatre. It was in the movie that I first heard this song and looked it up as I loved it. After he passed, I often listened to it and remembered my promise to him not to give up and to find love again. In a way, this song was a bit of a mantra for me. An encouragement and reminder not to give up and to keep believing that a second chance at love could be mine.

- "Near To You" by A Fine Frenzy

  o This is another song that came into my life through the Twilight movie saga. This song had a double meaning for me as many of the lyrics resonated with me around Cam and how I needed to be near to him. However, due to the inconsistency of our relationship at that time, it also was a song that gave me hope that one day there would be someone else who I was better near to even though I knew even then that there would never be a day I didn't love Cam. After Cam died and I met Kelsey, this song felt like it described the journey of navigating falling in love with one man while missing and loving another.

Appendix Nine:
My Journal, My Journey

"March 18, 2014

I never expected my body to come back so quickly while still grieving. It had been so long since I had felt a sexual inclination towards anyone, even Cam, and it had been even longer since Cam and I had been intimate. I had turned that part of me off, because it wasn't a possibility and I focused that energy elsewhere. I learned to love in deeper more meaningful ways than just sex. Yet within a week of him passing, my nights were filled with vivid dreams or recollections of Cam and I. And I'd wake feeling satisfied and yet yearning for him more then I possibly ever did when he was here. This subsided after a couple weeks and yet it left the desire to be touched, held, kissed, and wanted by another. God, I'm so confused, and have no idea what to do or what would be best. I love Cam more than I thought would be humanly possible and, if anything, my love for him has only grown since he left this earth. He was everything I ever wanted and I feel blessed to have called him mine, even if it was far shorter than we had hoped or expected. I am so scared of getting stuck in grief, of the stories I hear from others about how they know someone who never was the same, never recovered after their loss. I have promised myself I will not be that person; I will push myself out of my comfort zone to ensure I am not that person. But that is so much easier said than done. It would have been far easier to just stay in bed with the blankets pulled up and cried or been numb, but that isn't me even if I want to be that way. So no, I have forced myself to get active again, take care of my dogs, see friends, and reach out to people every single day. I have decided that I have no reason for feeling guilty when I flirt or entertain thoughts that a couple months ago would have been inappropriate in my opinion for a married woman to have. I want to feel alive and fuck it if that means doing things outside of the normal or expected way for a widow to grieve. I know what Cam and I shared was amazing, and anyone who was witness to that should also know it. Therefore, if anyone dares question my love for Cam based on how fast I choose to move on, then we can have that conversation. For if they do, they have either never lost a partner and do not know the depths of devastation which can force you to seek comfort in ways you may never have expected, or well, they just aren't me. So I'm back and forth, totally wanting to find someone, believing and feeling like I really am or at least should give it a try, and then a sobbing mess because how can I ever look for what I had with Cam with someone else? And maybe it will never be what I had with him, maybe it will be just as wonderful but in different ways. And maybe, just maybe, that will be okay. But I just don't know and that is terrifying."

"March 24, 2014

Nothing prepares you for when their gone. I was grieving and getting counseling every week the whole way through since his diagnosis and yet the emptiness when he went was like nothing I could have ever imagined. And thank goodness I didn't know how bad it would be so I could just be with him and focus on having fun or laughing with him rather than always crying. And that's where I am again today. I have kept myself so busy since he passed and over the last week have gotten good at distracting myself, but today I thought I'd give myself a day to relax. Well, it ended up being a day to just cry and cry, which I guess is just where I'm at and okay. But I just don't understand how my emotions are all so raw and intense. Cam really wanted me to not roll over when he went, to grieve but get back out there and live life, to look for someone else to fulfill my dreams with because he just couldn't stand the thought of me alone. And on a day like today, I just can't imagine ever having what I had with him, can't imagine feeling more comfortable in my own skin while with him than I even did alone. But strangely there are days where I shock myself, where I do feel like I'm moving along and where I can tell stories and laugh without crying. There are days I even think about dating and being in a relationship, where I will talk about hoping to meet someone to have kids with. And yet I feel horrible that I already am thinking this way on occasion. How can he only be gone for just over a month and I'm already planning the next phase of my life? But I don't feel ready for a relationship, I only want Cam, yet can't have him, and I still want to be wanted. I just don't know how to trust myself, because some days I'm a sobbing mess and know I still need to fully grieve before getting involved with someone else. But then there are other days where I don't feel so bad and actually feel alive and like I can survive this."

"March 30, 2014

Today I looked around my house and decided I should take down all the pictures of us. Just get rid of them. Well not rid of, but put them in a box and put them away. But what would I put up instead? Should I keep the frames but remove the pictures? The frames that hold our wedding pictures were all quite expensive and it would be a shame to put them in a box after only having them up for 8 months. So maybe I should keep the frames where they are, but take out the pictures and put in new ones. Yet after over 5 years of being with my favorite person in the world, what the hell would I fill all these beautiful frames with? There are barely any pictures without him in it or where he wasn't the photographer, and thus remind me of him. And can I stand to see the frames I picked with Cam holding pictures other than us, when they used to hold memories of so many amazing times we had? I can't imagine my home without these pictures. I can hardly still believe that my husband no longer lives here in his physical body with me. So I realize that today is not the day to take down the pictures, that I'm simply not ready for it and that that is okay. I'll know when I'm ready and maybe it will be one picture at a time, maybe it will be in one swoop. I don't need to know today even though I want to."

"March 31, 2014

Looking back I'm so grateful I got to marry Cam. Nothing, no pain and not death can take those memories from me. I had no idea what 'in sickness or health' would mean or how much I would be tested by those vows, but I would do it all again in a heartbeat. Watching your love disappear and suffer, and not being able to do anything other than sit with them, cook, bathe and always love them is horrifying. It is exhausting and yet there is no time to be exhausted because they need you. And no one else around you gets it, because they don't live it day in and out. I was cheated from a long lifetime of happiness, and it's just not fair. I went to a thrift store yesterday and bought all the cheap plates I could find. Then, with a sharpie, wrote on the plates all the things I had lost, all the anger, and sadness. I plan to go to the dump and smash them and scream. Just let it all out.

I've come to realize there is no preparing for it, for the end. My greatest blessing is I have no regrets. There are intense moments of sadness, but there are also moments of relief. I went for my first walk on my own two weeks after he passed and I remember realizing that there was no need to bring the cell phone, no need to stay close, no need to worry. The worst had happened and I was still breathing, struggling to breathe at times, but I was still here. Living in an hour glass is not for the faint of heart. Strangely the pain changes after your love dies. It became about me and not so much about feeling powerless to help him."

"April 2, 2014

I recognize that partly I'm angry. I had wondered when this part of the grieving process would visit me. I'm angry that he had to leave me, that my plans to spend the rest of MY life with him were not followed and some other grand plan took precedence. And it is likely that anger that makes me want to just go through my house and get rid of everything that reminds me of him, because even if it's all around, it doesn't change that he's not. I just feel like I'm pretending that one day he will come home. I love the denial but also know I can't have it, that it's really not even there anymore. There is no denying that he has passed on. So what is the fucking point of having all these pictures up, of a life I don't get to partake in, of a life I wanted so bad I was willing to do anything to have it and yet here I am without it? I can't seem to take my wedding rings off and yet feel foolish every time I look at them. I never knew it would be possible to have so many conflicting emotions all at exactly the same time. I cling to the days I feel better, to the days I smile and laugh easily, to the days I feel him close to me and to the days where I feel my body come alive when I look or chat with other people because, to me, this signifies that I will be okay in time. I'm not right now and that's to be expected, but I'm coming alive again, I'm getting myself on the right track. There is no guide book for grief, or if there is, it doesn't always fully work. I have to do this my way, at my pace and sometimes that way is faster than others would expect or want, and at other times it's pretty damn slow with lots of steps backwards."

"April 4, 2014

I remember vividly the feeling of not knowing the person I was with on certain days. I remember after about a week of him not acting like himself I said to a friend I just wanted to put him against a wall, shake him and scream for the man I loved to come back out. When they are 'gone' it feels helpless, as there is nothing you can do but wait and hope for another chance to be with THEM again. Not sure why I'm remembering this today, but I guess it's just another way that I started to lose him in pieces even before he died. There were so many losses over the year and a half he was sick and yet it still didn't prepare me for him to be fully gone. Nothing can ever prepare you."

"April 7, 2014

Not only did I lose Cam, and that loss was more incomprehensible than can be described, but I lost my own identity which had come to be directly linked to my life with him. Nearly as devastating a loss as Cam was also the loss of our future together, of my expected and desired future. We had thousands of dreams, dreams we were only starting to manifest. I had expected to be his wife forever, to become a part of his family and continue being included in the family traditions while creating our own. But now the most important link is gone and nothing is guaranteed. How long does it take to be integrated into a family? Was I? Did I always want to be? And yet the thought of losing that last connection I had to Cam has been devastating and terrifying all on its own. This has become my family, No it was not perfect, but neither is my biological family. But what if it was only my family because of Cam? Now the obligation to include me is gone. These thoughts flag my mind and the potential future goodbyes I may be forced to make terrify me."

"April 12, 2014

I've come to realize that when grieving, you're heartbroken and trying to get through the day any way you can. And that's enough. We survive as best we can and sometimes to the outside world it doesn't look like we are doing a very good job. I despise the statement "you're not coping very well." I usually am pretty good at saying that I have my moments and some are better than others, but I feel like shaking my head and asking them exactly how they think I should cope. Feeling numb is so weird when the other emotions are so raw and in your face. But at least the other emotions let you know you are alive and here. Being numb is like being stuck in a twilight zone and watching yourself do things as if in a movie. Feeling far away from them or alone is the worst for me. It's eight weeks today since Cam passed and I panic when I realize I can't pull his voice into my head on my first try or fully remember what he smelt like. But I do remember how loved I felt. I remember the way he treated me and the way he would tease me with so much love and caring that it hardly seemed like teasing. I cling to those things and I go and sit in places that were special to him or us and I imagine myself hugging him. It helps, but it doesn't make it better. On a positive note, I am beyond proud of myself that yesterday was the third meal I have cooked since he passed and the first one I did fully on my own, grocery shopping and everything! It feels funny to celebrate the things that have been second nature to me for so long, but I have forgotten how to live in this world and am now just relearning everything."

"April 15, 2014

I read a quote by Elizabeth Harper Neeld in Seven Choices today that hit home "Freedom crashed down on me...But this was a freedom that I despised, a freedom that I didn't want, a freedom that frightened me. For this freedom was a form of emptiness, of nothingness" (p. 168). I had eagerly tied my life, dreams and goals to his. I put my life on hold to ensure his last days, weeks and months were as pleasurable as possible and I would do it all again. And yet here suddenly I am free from the obligations of being a wife; free from the exhausting pressure of being a caretaker. And this freedom means I am alone. I am free falling with no one to tie myself to, with no givens or structure to my days, nights, present or future. I did not choose this freedom, do not want this freedom. I would give anything for it to not be my reality. Yet it is."

"April 23, 2014

This is the first week where I feel any sort of relief at the past being over, with my job as a caretaker over and that I'm free to make my own plans and live my life how I want to, undictated by medical systems or someone else's needs. I would give anything for Cam to be healthy and to spend the rest of our lives together, but that didn't happen. I wanted very badly to be able to go on caring for him as things deteriorated and I often have said I would have done that forever if I could. That sacrificing my life would have been okay, because I got him and that was enough. In many ways that is true, I would have done anything for him, and I did, and I would have continued doing that. But now that it's been nine weeks, I realize I was more exhausted than I could have known and I couldn't have gone on forever, even if I had wanted to. So yes, I miss him with every ounce of my being and some days still feel like the most vital part of me is missing, but I'm starting to see myself as separate from him, as my own person. I'm finding my own way. And I'm enjoying it. I'm almost grateful that the caretaking is over, but it's hard to say that without feeling like I'm saying that I'm grateful he is dead and that's not the case at all. But I'm grateful for where I'm at now and how well I'm doing."

"May 4, 2014

Well, today is a very hard day for me. I was worried my birthday would be hard and so I had ensured I would be busy all day and night. But I hadn't really thought about the day after. It's amazing how when it hits, it's like a ton of bricks and I can't breathe. I just miss him so much and would give anything to just hold him. There are a few things that set me off this time, I think, or at least are making it more intense. I got my period in the middle of the night and that impacts my mood. I got drunk last night and have always been emotionally unstable afterwards, which was actually partly why Cam hated being around me the next day when we did drink. He would complain that I would be super clingy. And now I feel that way, but there is no one to hold. And I just wish he was alive, I miss him so much! Cam is all I want, all I've ever wanted, since he came into my life. But I can't have him, not in the ways I want him and that's hard to accept. I just hate being alone."

"May 11, 2014

Reaching, searching, growing ever so slowly it is hardly recognizable to the naked eye. At times the energy is used up simply trying to keep going, keep smiling and getting better. The sun continues to shine, the world continues to turn and with it I change, yet it is hard to understand or accept this change, hard to get comfortable in my own skin. I know what works, I've done this long enough, but it takes work and dedication to bring out my happy side, my true essence. The rain isn't pleasant, it feels like temporarily my growth has stopped, but in truth, without it, growth would not be possible. So I embrace and accept all events, all emotions as they present themselves. No, I do not enjoy them but I realize it is all part of the growing. Growing has always been painful; it was when I was little and could feel my legs stretching a little longer and it is now as my heart and spirit expand. My dogs provide consistency and the semblance of routine and they reward me with complete love. The gym provides community and self-love. I know the members and am embraced as I come in, welcomed and questioned on my absence, not judgmentally but out of caring. I leave feeling full, feeling accomplished, feeling better about myself, because I put myself first. Connection, learning to not only reach out to others, but to also allow them to be a part of my life. I haven't needed others for so long, not really or at least the ways I needed them they couldn't really help with most of the time. Now I just want connection, just want their love and presence. That is enough and leaves me feeling full and cared for. They do not know how much their friendship means, nor could they, even though I gush with gratitude. I see the fear that they are not doing enough or that they don't know what to say, see them pull away for fear of doing/saying something wrong. But they couldn't or even if they do it doesn't matter. I forgive them as we are all walking in unchartered territory. I just don't want to walk alone and, luckily, I don't have to."

"May 20, 2014

I looked at my finances and realized that I can't afford this house on my own. That if I want to keep my home, the home that Cam declared when we saw it just a year ago, the one he could picture spending the next 20 years in, then I would have to get roommates. Roommates. I thought I had outgrown that stage of my life. I think of having roommates as a rite of passage for young adults going to University or just starting out. I had assumed that if Cam and I were ever to live with another person it would be our child, not a stranger. And yet here I am organizing the office, Cam's office, his music studio. I hadn't realized how much he had crammed in that room. There are a ridiculous amount of video games, so many instruments and recording devices, and somehow five computers. What do I do with all these things he loved so much? I will not have room to store them, nor do I have any need for them. And yet he loved them all. I remember when he bought or was given so many of these items, remember the excitement he had. I had always known we would be clearing out this room, but I thought it would be with Cam's help and because a baby was on the way. I had always figured we would have arguments over what had to go versus stay, but that the argument was because our family was growing and that the excitement of that would overpower everything else. But now there is no excitement. And Cam isn't with me. I'm alone and opening the doors to our home to a complete stranger, because if I don't, then I can't stay here. And if I can't stay here, then I can't keep my dogs, and that is simply not an option. So I let the tears come, I angrily look at all that I have left of Cam and I sort through it, and I resent every second of it."

"June 1, 2014

It is amazing how after a few months I can still be hit by random things that remind me that Cam is gone. I looked at Bentley today, asleep on his dog bed, and noticed his dog tag, which still has Cam's and my number on it. Cam's number is now disconnected, it no longer exists, just as he no longer exists. It is the small things that hurt so bad and hit home the hard reality of just how much has changed."

"June 15, 2014

It still amazes me how people judge, and how easily it comes out without them even thinking about the impact it might have on me. It is their opinion, and yes, they are allowed to have it but, my God, use a filter! And I know I'm overly sensitive, an unreturned phone call can suddenly turn into me being afraid that they think I'm too needy and I regularly create stories out of nothing. This I know because I watch myself do it all the time. But at times I'm pretty sure it's just plain judgement. I told some people about how excited I was that I found some art work to put up in the living room to replace all the wedding pictures. Rather than encouragement, I was met with "Why would you want to do that? You haven't even had them up very long to enjoy them. That's just too soon." I respond that I'm not technically married anymore so having wedding pictures up seems kind of silly. I then get to hear about how gorgeous they are, as if I didn't know that already, and am reminded of how much work Cam and I went through to get them and the money they cost. I felt like saying, "Yes, it has been short and we did go through a lot to get them. It's unfortunate he died a few months later and all I'm left with are gorgeous magazine worthy pictures on my walls." Like seriously, I LOVE my wedding pictures and they look amazing in my house, but what they represent is no longer. This is also something I have agonized over for hours since he died. Do I leave them up? Do I just put different pictures in the frames? Do I buy new pieces completely? What do I do with the frames? The pictures? No one could possibly know how much it pains me to think about putting them away. But I don't need judgement. I need responses like, 'Oh, what is the art of?', or 'Wow that's a big step, how are you doing with it?' I don't want to have to rationalize or explain my reasons to others because I already have gone over it all with myself a hundred times. I want, no need, this to be my home. Cam isn't coming through the front door ever again. He is dead and nothing I do can change that. Keeping pictures up doesn't make it easier or change it. He will always be in my heart, I will always turn to him for advice and guidance but that's inside me, no matter where I am or what my home looks like. This is still 'our' home and in a way always will be, but just like when we moved in and changed some of the floors, painted, put up new light fixtures and decorated to make it feel like our home, I now need to do little things to make it feel like mine. I guess I have to understand not everyone will understand; indeed they can't unless they have been there and even then we all react differently."

"June 30, 2014

It's interesting when I objectively stand back and watch my brain try to conceptualize that Cam has passed. It's still a hard concept to accept and understand the reality and finality of. I haven't cried in my sleep that I remember in a while now, yet last night I dreamt in explicit detail, not so much of Cam dying, but the days that followed; the realization that he was gone, how alone I felt, the waves of agonizing sorrow that engulfed me. I dreamt of all the pain I had gone through, of being with my siblings and dad afterwards and the intense pain of it all. My poor brain is still trying to catch up, to make sense of what I saw, what I went through and am still going through. As light and good as I felt yesterday, as much closure I felt after scattering his ashes, there is still the strange reality that Cam's body, which I loved so much, had kissed and touched every part of, was reduced to ashes. That I held my love in my hands and watched him float away on the breeze. That is a strange thing to wrap your head around. And so I dreamt of the intense sadness I feel at finding myself in this situation and I woke myself from the heaving sobs and soaked pillow. Slowly my brain and heart will come to terms with it, but there will be hiccups along the way I'm sure."

"July 28, 2014

Not sure where the last couple of weeks have gone. They have been hard, I miss Cam a lot lately. Had my estate/yard sale this weekend and it actually wasn't as bad as I had been worried it would be. Getting ready for it was super hard and has been brutally emotional. Every item has a memory, a story, a fight, laugh, conversation attached to it. And I felt it was healthy and important to allow myself to remember all of that rather than avoid or rush through. So I cried lots and lots, sobbed as I held each thing before putting it in a box to be sold, sobbed as I cleaned up the TV room in the basement so that my second roommate can put her things down there. All his lovely art supplies, many of which he never used. Both of our year books with messages for the future, a future that has been cut short. People's hopes for us, which now will never be fulfilled. Cam had been so happy that I had a place to put my sewing material and bought me a table so that the TV room could second as my sewing room. All the dreams and plans we had, we were making and living. The wedding pictures that lined the wall. Taking each of them down was super hard, and I sobbed with each frame because I know they will never go back up. It's really over, my time as a married woman is over, for now at least, and I fear forever. I'm lonely. I miss Cam, miss my best friend and husband, but I also miss what he represented. I miss having someone I can rely on. I don't really have that with anyone else. And I miss feeling really wanted by someone I also want. Sometimes it feels like I'm destined to be alone forever."

"August 5, 2014

There is no one else to turn to. There is no waiting to do a certain chore with hopes that they do it before you're forced to. No division of the chores within the home or yard. It's just me and only me unless I want to hire someone, and then it's still my responsibility to determine who to hire and pay them. There is being alone and missing another's presence. Then there is the disbelief that you'll

288

never hear their voice again, never feel their touch. There is how much you miss them deep down in your core. And, of course, there is the heart wrenching loss of all the dreams we had together, of the plans that will not be ours to share. But there is also an overwhelming sense of sudden responsibility, of suddenly being IT. No longer a pair; simply one, alone, single, all that is left."

"September 2, 2014

When Cam first died, living without him didn't feel like living at all. I didn't want to live without him. But over the last few months I have learned more than I ever could have about my ability to survive, my ability to inspire, my determination to make a difference, to honor myself and others, especially Cam. I've learned to appreciate being alive and to appreciate each breath I'm blessed with. I learned to take care of me and to love me the same way I want to be loved, the same way I loved Cam and he loved me back. The things that are truly important have been put into perspective. I never would have learned all of these things if Cam hadn't died. I was focused on him and lost myself. This happened right at the start when he was drinking; then we became a united WE in sobriety and lost our individuality. I wanted this, loved it but now am starting to realize it wasn't good for me. I realize I always gave Cam credit for any growth I did and, in a way, it was true he has been my greatest teacher, my catalyst for change. But all my learnings since his death have been fully me. Sure, he has helped from the other side as have many of my friends and family. But it has been my choice each and every day to keep going and I had to decide how to then get through each day. It has been my choice to survive, to love myself, to cry, to laugh and to allow my heart to be open to loving again, to really honor my dreams even if they didn't turn out as I had expected or with the person I thought they would. I learned a lot about what kind of person I am and to no longer live in fear because I have faced the unimaginable and survived."

"September 8, 2014

I remember and, well, in honesty, it's still there, the intense feeling of being afraid of being judged by others. I wanted to 'grieve properly' as if there is such a thing. And, well, I really don't want to hurt others or make their grieving journey any harder. When I feel people's judgement come on, I get angry, as they have no right. They do not know what it feels like to roll over onto a cold spot on the bed, what it feels like to stare at a toothbrush that logically you know you should throw out because it will never be used again; yet somehow that would be admitting he was truly never coming back. They didn't see the tears that flowed from my eyes, no one knew how much I cried that day or all the days that have followed. He is physically gone, yet I am forced to carry on. He went the one place he made me promise again and again that I wouldn't follow. This is my life and while I would give anything to have spent it with him; would give anything to hear his contagious laugh, see his mischievous smile, kind eyes and feel his warm touch, I know that somehow he understood before he died what I was going to be asked to endure. He understood better than I did even at that time how hard losing him would be. And he loved me, loved me in the most unselfish way possible and for that he made me promise to eventually move on without him, to fulfill our dreams with someone else. It is why he not only gave me permission, but made me promise, I would choose to open my heart to love again, as he knew I would be here and he would not."

"December 5, 2014

The last few days have been extra difficult or I guess I should say have returned to being difficult. It's strange, the ache and longing in my heart is always there, he is present in eighty percent of my thoughts at any given time, but it has become normal most days. I live life and go about my days. I don't forget, but it's no longer like I can't breathe, like I'm drowning. And then there are the waves of grief that rake through my body and mind, that threaten to crush me. That make it feel raw and new again, as if I just lost him or am in the process of losing him all over again. In so many ways he is still here, I haven't lost him. Yet I lost the ability to hold him, to feel his touch, to see his eyes twinkle, to hear his laugh or voice. I lost the future we dreamed of having together. He won't be in the delivery room or get the chance to hold our child. I don't think there ever will be an 'our child' unless I choose to use his sperm I have frozen. I can still talk to his spirit and sometimes I can almost hear his responses and feel his presence. But it's not the same and I miss him so very much. I can't believe that it's been four years since Cam asked me to marry him. So much has happened since then. I still can't help but laugh at how he actually managed to find a way to surprise me. I don't know why I was so controlling of how or when he asked me to marry him. I guess I wanted a non-embarrassing perfect story to tell people and I didn't trust him to do something romantic. It's sadly funny that I was so focused on how he would ask me to marry him so that I could have a great story to tell people and now no one will likely ever ask how he asked me to be his wife. It is a story like so many others that seems awkward and sad to share, which doesn't seem appropriate to bring up at happy moments when others are telling their engagement stories. But I'll never forget. I'll treasure that feeling of shock, disbelief and pure excitement. I remember it all and I guess I'll just have to be grateful I have the memories to hold and cherish."

"January 9, 2015

I want to be free of all responsibility and to be accountable to no one. I want to be able to go and come as I please without concern for who I may be affecting with my actions. Yet I equally fear and desperately run away from this very desire. I claim that had I not had dogs when Cam died, that I would have packed up and went travelling. In truth, I do not know what I would have done. There is the chance fear of the future would have been enough for me to take my life, as thoughts of suicide were unyielding those first few weeks and even months. Maybe I would have travelled and given up my job and maybe that would have been best, or maybe it would have left me feeling even more alone. It is hard to look back on our choices and judge how things would have been different/better, for we can never know. This is not a "choose your own adventure" book; this is my life, real life. I could still go, but I do not know where I desire and in a way it is not simply a trip or vacation I long for. No, it is to run from the life I created. But I also very much want this life, when it felt taken from me when Cam died I began to search for ways to find balance and harmony in order to create it again. I want to be a wife, I want to be a mother, I want to own dogs and own a pretty home. I want to know that I am the first thing another human being thinks of when they awake. I want to long for another and have that longing met over and over again. So yes, I long for the freedom of only having responsibility for myself, but I fear the loneliness I know accompanies it. And my greatest fear, the fear of growing old alone outweighs all other desires."

"January 24, 2015

I am grateful for my home, for this house that keeps me warm and dry. I feel safe in here, like it is my own personal sanctuary. I look at how nice my furniture is, how well put together it is and I feel proud. Yet it tells of a story that not everyone might know. This place is different than my first spot, my condo. The condo had hand me down furniture and mismatched plates and cutlery. It was filled with garage sale things, but I loved it and it was mine. This home is all new other than my dining room table. It speaks of promises and dreams. The couches and coffee tables we fell in love with and my dad paid for, laughing that we have nicer furniture than he ever has had. The real silver cutlery that was ridiculously expensive and our incredibly lovely dinner set. Everything in my home screams 'newlyweds'. All the random appliances I'll only use on occasion. I love them all, wanted and still want them all, yet I don't have the person I want it all with. I don't have the person I picked them all out with. And I'm reminded of that every day."

"April 10, 2015

I had Easter dinner at my place and it went wonderfully. It was so easy and I felt really and truly happy. There was lots of laughing and a carefreeness to it. And yet, I kept having these simultaneous thoughts about how lovely this was with everyone over, and then at the same time there was an ache and sadness at the realization that there will likely never be a family gathering with Cams family again at my home. That the chapter where it is Cam's family, we or even I am hosting, is finished. And the happier I get in my current life, the more I walk away from the bridge that spans my life with Cam. The happier I become, the more I realize he is really and truly gone and I'm carrying on somehow. It's a good thing and exactly what he would want, told me he wanted, but it's still weird that I had planned my forever with this person who now is gone and not coming back. I carry him with me always, but I'm back to living in the present with my new boyfriend and beginning to dream of our future together. I no longer spend as much time living in the past and that's healthy, but still strange and new for me. I guess I've entered a new chapter in my life, one where Cam comes with me, but is no longer the main character.

Made in the USA
Monee, IL
13 December 2021

84320675R00164